For my sons, Charlie & Smith.

Everything happens for a reason . . . we make up afterwards.

The RESPONDENT

A True Story

*Exposing the Cartel
of Family Law*

Greg Ellis

LOS ANGELES/ VIRGINIA BEACH/ CAPE CHARLES

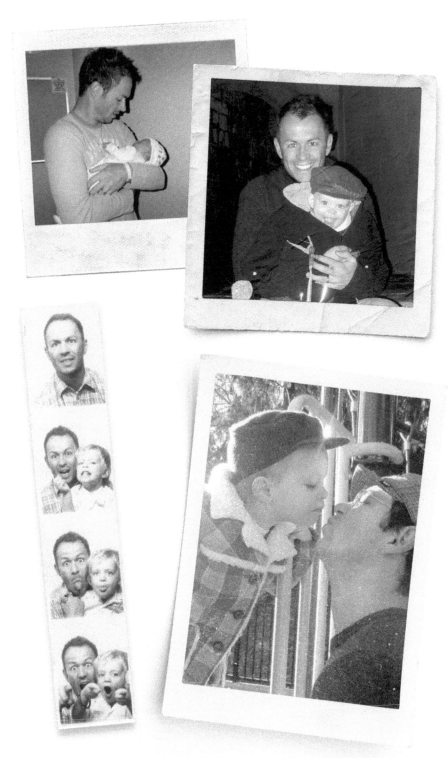

TABLE OF CONTENTS

DEDICATION

The Respondent is both a chilling reminder and essential therapy for anyone navigating the recrimination and trauma that is modern American divorce. It is also both diagnosis and prescription, meditating on the depths of the crisis and the way out.

Greg Ellis sets the record straight and shatters the myths of divorce court. This is Greg's story. It's your story. And it's our story.

If you're trapped in the dungeon that is the family court system, *The Respondent* should be your constant companion.

—Johnny Depp

FOREWORD

A friend of mine recently announced to our small group of friends that he is getting divorced. He had murmured, over the past several years, that he and his wife had been, essentially, living separate lives for some time. I had viewed his marriage with more than a little doubt. However, as is so often the case, when the moment arrived, there was general *dismay*, even sadness. My friend had meditated a good deal about the positive consequences of leaving his marriage. The day his wife told him, and for a while after, he vacillated between joy and grief.

No normal, healthy human being goes into a marriage fixating on its failure. In my own case, even while I knew my life would improve once extricated from my first marriage, when the endgame began, I felt defeated and overwhelmingly reflective. Divorce is the death of a union, a family, a living thing.

In the ensuing years, as I was dragged through the suffering and humiliation of the California family law system (an entity that I came to equate with a criminal organization, defined by their casual willingness to inflict pain in order to extort money), I became outraged by what I was put through. So much so that I wrote a book about the experience.

Nearly every individual who enters into a contentious custody battle is unprepared for the attendant bitterness and acrimony, the lion's share of which is exacerbated or manufactured by lawyers. There's little money in a swift, collaborative divorce. And divorce lawyers, as well as the judges who serve their interests, know full well that most parents will do what is necessary to protect their relationship with their children. And they will also spend whatever is necessary, within their means, to navigate this corrupt system.

Reports from the front lines of custody battles are ubiquitous. That does not lessen their significance nor their value in the lives of someone you know who may, one day, find themselves in need of the guidance such tellings provide.

It is in this spirit that I encourage you to read Greg Ellis's book, *The Respondent*, a fresh and updated take from an American divorce court, where some things have changed (now men are seeking—and in some instances even gaining—sole custody of their children, either justifiably or as the result of the malignant parental alienation that plagued them for so long) and some things are, unconscionably, the same.

Divorce court, divorce mediation, custody evaluations, forensic accountings . . . it's all a foreign land to most people and one where you can easily lose your sanity coming to terms with the senseless rules that govern there, rules that will potentially affect the rest of your life.

You will need help. This book is it.

—Alec Baldwin

PRELUDE

Fate is fickle.

A simple, three-word cliché that describes the fragility of our lives and the speed with which everything we think is real can become an illusion. Before March 5, 2015, this simple truth was little more than a philosophical abstraction for me. I appreciated its implications. But I'd never experienced it, never endured a dramatic and unforeseen shift in fortune that I could not navigate—until that fateful day six years ago.

One moment I was a successful actor and producer living in an expansive Hollywood home with my wife of twenty years and two young sons I adored. But everything changed with a knock on the door by police, the first engagement in a battle with America's unscrupulous and unstoppable family law cartel that has raged on for years and left me with scars, my family in ashes, and my boys without a father.

This book emerged from this devastating experience. Part memoir, part meditation, part manifesto, *The Respondent* is the story of my fall from grace—including the many ways I was the author of my own demise—and my consequent descent into despair and confusion as I was ushered through the gauntlet of the suffocating family law system.

But it's also the story of a slow emergence and rising. An awakening, both intellectually and emotionally, and ultimately, a catharsis. James Hollis, in opening *The Eden Project: In Search of the Magical Other*, describes this journey from tragedy to self-awareness like this: "In Greek tragedy, one feels the earth shudder when a protagonist claims complete self-knowledge. At that moment one may be certain that the gods begin their work—to stun the person back to the proper humility of Socratic questioning."

The spirit in those words lit in me a fire of curiosity that has brought me to uncomfortable truths, not only about myself, as I exorcise many of the demons that have clipped at my heels for decades, but about society at large. I believe America is in the grips of an epidemic that rages in plain sight and yet remains invisible to so many. The shocking reality is that 4,000 children are being ripped from their parents in American courtrooms every day, 1 in 3 children doesn't live with their biological father in the home, and 40 percent of those children haven't seen their fathers in more than a year. The fabric of society fraying as an unfeeling $60-billion-a-year family law system perpetuates the tragedy.

Fathers have a reputation for stoicism that belies a more complex reality in which we feel the pain of family separation every bit as deeply as mothers, a reality made clear by a grim statistic I restate more than once in *The Respondent*. Fathers who have become ensnared in the divorce system kill themselves eight times more than mothers. Pause and let that sink in for a moment. For every child who loses their mother to suicide during or after divorce, eight children lose their father. This is nothing short of a national health emergency demanding an honest accounting of the conditions driving such despair.

The Respondent is not intended as a vehicle for vindictiveness. But I believe we are all willing participants in a shameful, social kabuki dance, mindlessly fortifying the most destructive narrative of our era—that women, merely by virtue of being women, are the fairer sex. I realize this is provocative to many in our current social climate. But before jumping to judgment, I hope you'll come with me as I visit not only the darker side of my story but also the shadow of our collective psyche in an attempt to answer this question: What is driving us to devalue fathers and family and perpetuate such a draconian divorce system?

When I walked into a dreary courtroom in downtown Los Angeles for the first time more than half a decade ago, I passed from a world of rights and justice to a star chamber of withering and reflexive judgment where due process is extinct and the presumption of innocence is an illusion. In crossing the legal Rubicon from citizen to pre-judged villain, I no longer occupied the skin of a complicated human being. Greg Ellis was dead, and in his place stood the nameless Respondent, present only to receive the slings and arrows of a society determined to exact its pound of flesh in retribution for male sin writ large.

The Respondent is my humble submission to the struggling dialogue. My hope is that you find it to be many things at once: a white-knuckled ride through a dirty swamp, an intimate inquiry into love and separation, an exploration of my failings as a modern man and my trauma as a boy, and a helpful (if incomplete) map pointing to a more humane and collaborative future, not only for forsaken fathers searching for redemption and justice, but for the whole village of people who love them: aunts, uncles, cousins, grandmas, and grandpas. If we are to fashion a better world for our children, there is no more urgent project than rebuilding divorce court, revitalizing the image of family, and recasting fatherhood as the foundational and heroic role of a lifetime.

We have all been *The Respondent*—the person summoned to respond to the allegations of a petitioner or the provocations of our times. This book is my legacy petition. I am *The Respondent*. And this is my story.

PART ONE

FEAR

"I'm sick of this shit.
I'm gonna harm the children."

CHAPTER 1

THE NOCTURNAL TERRORIST

"If the eyes have no tears, the soul has no rainbow."

My body is limp and naked but for a thin, sullied sheet strewn around my waist. I'm on my back, my arms hang outstretched in a submissive crucifixion. My hair is matted and caked with dried blood around my right ear, my eyes clenched shut with fear.

The downpour is relentless.

Then my body flinches, my nostrils flare. Small expressions pop and twitch as I recover consciousness. The invisible straitjacket of sleep paralysis loosens. The dream recedes.

And then my nightmare begins.

Desperately parched, I pry open my cracked lips to take in the water, only to be shocked by its bitterness. My senses now tripped into awareness, I peer up and shock turns to disgust as it dawns on me that the rain is cascading from a penis protruding from a tangled forest of pubic hair. A naked man is pissing on my face.

I can't avoid the gruesome reality confronting me any longer. I am no longer a man with a family and a career forged over forty years of toil and triumph. I am now but an inmate sprawled in a bed of a dark holding cell, a scrap of tissue stuck to the boot of a legal system as foreign to me as a distant universe.

What a difference a day makes. I wouldn't blame you for not believing that—a mere twenty-four hours before my unwitting experience as a human toilet—I was pitching a project to a Hollywood studio head, meeting with Joe Pesci and Andy Garcia, chatting it up with Sharon Stone and playing golf with Adam Levine, all before strumming my two sons to sleep on a ukulele in my beautiful Los Angeles mansion. You also could be forgiven for not understanding why—instead of striking back at the unspeakable violation with all the fury I could muster to reclaim at least a shard of dignity—I lay my head back down, shut my eyes, and submitted to the degradation in full.

Reclamations would come, but only after many years of my self-respect being starved, stripped, and assaulted, and endless efforts to uncover who I really am and how I wound up here.

But for the moment, with no reserves left, I would accept the piss.

• • •

My fall into oblivion had started eight hours earlier at around 3:30 PM on March 5, 2015. My wife, Dana, was out of state on a business trip and I had given the nanny the afternoon off so I could spend quality time with our two boys. Charlie was ten at the time, Smith eight. Everything seemed so normal. We were laughing and joking in the playroom when the doorbell rang. I walked down the stairs, opened my front door, and found myself face to face with two police officers from the LAPD.

"We received a call about your sons. Are they here?"

What a strange question, I recall thinking. Why would the police be at my doorstep, seemingly randomly, asking about my sons?

"We just need to know they are safe."

"Yes. They are upstairs. I can assure you they are safe."

"Sir, we received a call that you threatened to harm your sons."

"That's nonsense. Who called you?"

"That's confidential information. We just need to know they are safe, sir."

"Confidential? If I'm to be accused of making threats to my sons, I'd like to know who's making the allegation. Who called you? What danger are they supposed to be in?"

They were silent. I was baffled and unsettled—who could possibly have called the police to report that I'd threatened my boys? We stood there for a moment, locked in a bizarre standoff, an ominous look in the eyes of the officers garrisoning my door. Hoping to break the impasse, I moved again to defuse the situation, reassuring them that my sons were fine and that there was no reason for concern. Uncomfortable with the simmering hostility and sensing there was nothing left to discuss, I reached to shut the door. But one of the cops stepped on the threshold to keep the door from fully closing, and the first pangs of genuine anxiety struck. I didn't know it then, but I had already migrated miles away from the world of suburban comfort that was mine just minutes before.

A shudder moved through me. Like midnight canaries in a coal mine, my mind went cold and my heart darkened. Panic was setting in, and I responded by gripping ever tighter to routine. I began making dinner for the boys, hoping that the act of domestication would calm the gathering storm. It didn't. The police did not enter through the open door; instead, they meandered around my lawn in what felt like a predatory sortie. I thought, if I remained calm and measured and demonstrated normalcy, the police would surely realize their time was better spent elsewhere.

As the police began circling, my friend Patrick Fabian arrived, and I took immediate solace in the fact that someone else would assure the police of my benevolence. Patrick checked on the boys upstairs and reported to the officers that both Charlie and Smith were fine. But his reassurance fell on deaf ears—the officers responded with barely a shrug.

My stomach tightened. In the kitchen, I discussed the situation with Patrick and, after a few minutes, returned to the front door, determined to reason with the police. But there would be no reason, no negotiation. To the contrary, at that moment a sergeant walked up the garden path to join his fellow officers, bringing the assembly of law enforcement crowding my front door to five officers in total.

The newly arrived sergeant took his turn interrogating me about Charlie and Smith's physical wellbeing, and my plaintiff response betrayed a mounting frustration.

"Sergeant, I've made no threats to my sons. They are safe, playing upstairs, and there's a witness who's corroborated that fact. You have no warrant, so please leave my property. I would like to know who called and lied about me threatening them."

The sergeant cleared his throat. "Sir, we received a call. You were reported to have said, "I'm sick of this shit, I'm gonna harm the children."

Ten short words—barely a sentence. And yet, strung together they formed a horrendous falsehood that was about to change my life forever.

It defied belief. Someone couldn't seriously have called the police and told them I was a threat to my children. *It has to be a big mistake,* I tried to tell myself. And yet, beneath the shock, I sensed that someone had called the police and had lied about me. Not just any lie, but the worst, most carefully manufactured deceit.

The slowly developing interrogation continued, and, after a few hours of probing, the veneer of civility collapsed and the assembled force of officers broke the line and entered the house. They questioned me further, but that was a mere pretense. Before long, I was informed that a SMART (Systemwide Mental Assessment Response Team) from the DCFS (Department of Children and Family Services) was on their way.

Then I was handcuffed.

Somehow, I felt as if I was both wide awake and sleepwalking through this surreal moment. I stood in the living room of my California dream home that represented four decades of labor. My children were upstairs. Did they witness any of this?

My front door yawned at the manicured lawns, the bright lights of the interior spilling out past the handful of officers and onto the street where neighbors were doing a half-hearted job at hiding their morbid curiosity as they moved along the sidewalk at a snail's pace.

Then the DCFS arrived and supplemented the existing police force, establishing a preposterously large crew to restore law and order to a situation lacking in neither. They evaluated me for approximately half an hour. I answered all their questions honestly—too honestly, it would turn out. Suffice to say that the right to remain silent is pointless unless you keep your mouth shut, and anything you say will be misquoted, then used against you.

The DCFS agents, having interrogated me, left the room to compare notes with the police. I awaited their verdict, still holding onto a sliver of hope that this would end peacefully with me bidding the cadre of officials a good evening. Soon they returned, set three items in front of me, and told me to pick one to take with me.

Take with me where? They wouldn't tell me.

I was presented with a stark choice, one I had to make immediately. I could take my wallet, my phone, or a drink coaster with an image of my wife as a baby (a Christmas gift to her the previous year). I chose the coaster, and was soon ushered out of my home, essentially for the last time.

As I was led to an unmarked police car, my wrists burning from the shackles and my back in considerable pain from a recent surgery, Patrick agreed to watch my sons until Dana got home from the airport. I glanced up at Charlie's bedroom window to see his silhouette. I wondered if he would sleep, what nightmares might haunt him, and what he must have been thinking as he watched his father being led away in handcuffs.

• • •

Without offering a seatbelt, they drove me at breakneck speed, siren blaring, weaving through the Thursday night rush hour traffic of Highway 101, in and out and off and on the hard shoulder. The wild maneuvering buffeted me around so relentlessly that I eventually slid off the backseat and onto the floor. Wedged between the seat and the floor in the footwell, I was in agony, both physically and psychologically. I let out a guttural cry. The glass partition slid open.

"Please pull over and help me up."

No response.

"Where are you taking me? I did not and have never threatened my sons," I said from the floor.

"We're nearly there."

The glass partition slid shut.

I was jammed on the floor for another ten minutes until, mercifully, we stopped. As I was yanked out of the back, I caught a glimpse of a sign—UCLA Medical Center.

I was pulled to my feet and led inside like a common criminal. One of the officers checked in with reception while the other remained at my side. I continued pleading my innocence and asking why I had been detained.

The DCFS' silence, in the wake of my plea, was chilling. We sat for an excruciating hour before they led me to the emergency room area and told me to sit in the hallway, which I did for yet another hour with not another shred of information.

My thoughts turned to my wife, Dana, who suffered from panic attacks and was due back from her trip. She would find the allegations ridiculous and fight for my release. I worried about what our young sons would go through without Dad to sing them to sleep and make them feel safe. It was my responsibility, as their father, to provide them with a sense of security, and I was now powerless to protect them. How could a single phone call and its lie unleash all this damage in just a matter of hours?

As I waited for some sort of clarity or explanation, things only worsened. Instead of receiving enlightenment from someone—

anyone—I was stripped of my clothing, told to put on a gown, and led to a tiny room to give a urine sample. I looked at myself in the mirror. What stared back at me was a broken man, defeated and depleted, wrists red and bruised from the handcuffs, back spasming in pain, eyes animated by terror. The night caught up with me and I collapsed, slamming my head on the porcelain sink and crumpling onto the cold tile floor.

I lay semi-conscious on the ground, my head split open, blood trickling along the floor into a puddle. The timed light in the room clicked off and I fell into darkness. I peered hazily through the crack at the bottom of the door where the light shone through. My vision slid in and out of focus as I teetered on the brink of consciousness. There was loud banging on the door, but it faded as I struggled to stay awake. I rolled onto my back, pushed myself toward the corner of the room and, using the wall as leverage, willed myself upright. I swung my hands up in front of me toward the sink. I managed to get close enough for my fingers to grip the porcelain, and I pulled myself to a standing position, my body protesting the forced rigidity of being upright.

"What are you doing in there?" a DCFS officer yelled. The banging outside intensified.

I staggered, fell toward the door, and, in the same motion, turned the knob to unlock it before stumbling out. I was led to a nearby cubicle and instructed to sit and wait.

After an hour or so, still handcuffed, I was led to the rear entrance of the hospital and strapped to a gurney by two nameless men in white uniforms, who slid me unceremoniously into the back of an ambulance. I protested again.

"Where are you taking me? I have a right to know where you're taking me."

Again, silence.

The doors slammed shut and darkness descended on me, both inside and out. I was terrified beyond thought, stripped of clothing and control. My head pounded. My back ached. My wrists burned.

The ambulance eventually slowed to a stop. The back doors swung open and I saw a dimly lit compound with perimeter security fencing. They unloaded me from the ambulance and wheeled me toward the front gates. One of the orderlies swiped his security card over a keypad at the front door, and I was ushered into the stark building, through two more sets of doors, and down multiple cavernous corridors. It was deathly quiet but for the squeaking of the gurney's wheels. We passed through one last set of security doors, then turned into a mess room with tables and chairs. They finally removed the handcuffs and a rakish man with a clipboard appeared, suggesting he was about to take control of my forced incarceration.

I was petrified.

My protests continued, though their force waned as I faltered. "Where am I? Why am I here? I need to know my sons are all right. You can't just lock me up!"

"5150. Threatened his children," the DCFS officer casually remarked to the rakish man, who pushed the clipboard into my midriff and ordered me to sign.

There is something uniquely punitive about the burden of paperwork amid a personal trauma of this magnitude. I had been forcibly removed from my home, falsely accused of threatening my children, and I was about to be involuntarily admitted into what was clearly a mental facility. And yet, somehow there were still forms to complete, and the dreariness of its normalcy only emphasized the extraordinary circumstances—the bureaucratic state, in all its bland menace, taunting me, forcing me to stipulate my own subjugation.

For all that, I was too incoherent to decipher what was written on the document and far too traumatized to care. The orderlies in white took all my personal belongings (the coaster, my watch, and my wedding ring), and gave me a pillow and a bed sheet.

"Please, tell me where I am," I pleaded. Finally, an answer came.

"You're being admitted to Del Amo Psychiatric Hospital."

I had no idea where that was or why I was there. I had lost my orientation in the world, forgotten my place in it. I felt extinguished.

But the orders continued. I was told to stand. Through another door stood a short, robust man awash in facial hair, armed with a chunky set of keys hanging from his belt strap. I shuffled behind him wearing only the itchy, bloody gown, clutching my pillow and bedsheet. He led me into a stark, sterile holding space with two tiny, thick, barred windows and six beds that bore the look and feel of mortuary slabs. The one in the left corner was mine.

This small, rotund man in whose charge I was now placed—and who literally held the key to my fate—placed the plastic bag with my clothing into a little cubby in the wall. With that, he left the room and shut the thick, steel door behind him. I heard the jingle of his keychain, then the turning of the lock. He looked back through the frosted glass of the watch window. A flashlight assaulted my eyes.

"Go to sleep," he commanded.

I placed my pillow on the slab and lay down, unruffling the bedding over the bottom half of my body. I tried to slow my racing thoughts and my breathing so that I might settle in for sleep inside the nightmare.

But the terror and disbelief and confusion would not relinquish their hold. My senses were raw and heightened, but my mind was dull and confused in an unfamiliar way. When I had awakened that morning, I could never have imagined the day would lead me here, alone in a psych ward, considered some sort of menace by faceless authorities and trapped in a legal spiderweb I'd never dreamed of. I knew I wasn't crazy or a danger to myself or others—especially my children. Yet here I was, like R.P. McMurphy in *One Flew Over the Cuckoo's Nest,* the sane man trafficking among the ill, more convinced by the minute that this place could drive anyone to an emotional apocalypse.

Why? That nagging question persisted.

Why would someone make up such a story about me? I attempted to reconcile the impossible. Who hated me so much that they were willing to perpetuate this monstrous falsehood to the police and try and tear apart my family and career, and, most importantly, leave my sons without a father? I was with them on the day of their births, cutting their umbilical cords, embracing them, sharing the love and unbridled joy with my family and friends.

"I'm sick of this shit, I'm gonna harm the children."

Those ten words kept ringing in my ears. Their author had used them like a weapon and condemned me in the process. I wondered where he or she was on this same night, probably sleeping comfortably in their own bed.

Harm my children? Is there a greater assault on a man's integrity?

I finally, gratefully, fell into slumber.

It wasn't long after that I woke to that rain of piss, and fresh horrors beyond.

CHAPTER 2

THE ORDER OF RESTRAINT

"Ignorance is bliss until your life falls apart."

Eighteen hours earlier, March 5 had begun in starkly different circumstances. I awoke in the comfort of my sprawling home in the affluent community of Toluca Lake—just steps from Warner Brothers and Universal Studios—to a day that seemed poised with limitless potential. I strolled down the stairs that morning into a world most could only conjure in their dreams. I woke the boys, made them breakfast, packed their lunches, and dropped them off at school with the usual hugs and well wishes for the day. Arriving back at the house and into my home office by 8AM, I soon greeted Andy Garcia, who had walked from his own home not far from mine, to discuss various projects on which we could collaborate. My assistant brought us coffee and we breezily passed the time with standard Hollywood talk. During the meeting, Sharon Stone called to discuss another project we were developing.

Later in the morning, I had to run down to the studio to record a voiceover for a Disney cartoon series. I then met with my agent to discuss ideas for television shows, before heading to Lakeside Golf Club for a quick meeting with Joe Pesci to discuss writing and directing his next movie.

And yet the dream was an illusion, my outward bliss a façade. My emotional furnace in fact was running hot, untempered by the professional possibilities and superficial pleasantry of the day. Sleep has been a struggle my whole life, and with Dana out of town, I couldn't shut down. Psychological foreshocks were rumbling and my ability to control them was dwindling rapidly. Fissures cracked wider in my mind and a world that appeared so right felt so very wrong. For days, I had felt I was spiraling into uncharted territory. I was at the pinnacle of my professional life, but my personal life was faltering, and as I rushed home to prepare for my next meeting of the day, ideas on what I needed to do to stop the bleeding percolated in my brain. I sent Dana a text:

> **Me:** We need to make time to sit down tonight to talk, babe.
>
> I feel like we are ships in the night and it is really important for us to take stock of our lives and where we are at. We must find a way to make life easier for you and for you to feel valued. Let's embrace that tonight. Okay?
>
> **Dana:** You got it

Dana and I had been partners in a twenty-year marriage, and it didn't take a genius to realize that wasn't a promising response.

I then met my friend and colleague Adam Fogelson in the rarefied air of his office at STX, an innovative film studio created just a few months earlier. Adam had recently taken the helm after four years as the Chairman of Universal Studios, and he had agreed to meet about some projects we'd spoken loosely about working on. Twenty-three floors up, his office had a stunning panoramic view of the world he commanded. Everything in the office was exactly where it should be, reflecting both his discipline and dignity.

Just after noon, I walked into this Hollywood temple with Chris, assistant to Greg Ellis, successful and respected actor, writer, and producer. The problem was, unbeknownst to Adam or Chris, my demons, churning for so long, were now breaching the surface. I had barely slept in three days, and I walked in accompanied by a mine of emotional chaos.

Adam and Chris quickly sensed something was wrong. I was somewhat incoherent and overwrought. With every thought, a stream of staccato irrelevance followed as I dominated a sprawling meeting and blew past my half-hour time allotment. I offered almost nothing of value in a confused word salad, but Adam was decent as ever and tried to pull coherence from the chaos—to no avail.

I left the STX offices, aware that I was emotionally exhausted. I proceeded to walk home, so I could clear my head and make sense of what was happening and how I was feeling. I realized that I needed to embrace big changes and move toward a healthier and more constructive life.

Armed with this solidifying conviction, I arrived home and checked on the boys. I then walked to my office in an adjacent building, feeling tranquil for the first time in memory. I informed our nanny, Kia, that she could go home for the day: I decided to forgo any more work and spend the afternoon with my boys. I sat down with my sons to read them a story.

Then the phone rang. It was Dana's cell, which immediately struck me as odd. She rarely used the phone to reach me when she was out of town on business, so I answered with curiosity. She dispensed pleasantries and asked me what was going on, concerned because Kia had called and claimed I had fired her. Dana often got confused, having been diagnosed with panic disorder years earlier and so, being accustomed to bouts of irrationality and misinterpretation, I explained that I had simply told Kia she could have the rest of the afternoon off and by no means had I fired her. I later realized there was a sharp edge to Dana's voice during the call, but it barely registered at the time. I promised to text Kia and clear up the misunderstanding, which I did immediately, then handed the phone to our eldest son Charlie, thinking the barely perceptible blip in our day had been sorted.

Charlie said a few words and then, with a quizzical look, told me, "Mom's hung up." Strange, perhaps, but hardly alarming. Quickly moving past the call, I returned to story time with the boys. We were laughing, joking, and singing in the playroom when the doorbell tolled.

A mere few hours later, I became a human toilet in a place reeking of dread and pathology. My passive response to the urination assault emboldened the stranger relieving himself on me, so that when I finally reacted, he attacked, and I took two blows to the face before I was able to fend him off. The commotion woke the other patients, and the staff rushed in to tear him off me and take him away.

I was filthy, battered, and bloodied. A foreign feeling of dread clung to my shoulders.

"You got it," Dana's last text read. But I didn't get it. Not at all. That night was March 5, 2015, and it was just the beginning of a dystopian nightmare that still envelops me today. My two boys have not shared bedtime with me since that night. They were ten and eight years old then. They are now seventeen and fourteen. I have missed over half a decade of their childhoods.

And so, those ten false words—"I'm sick of this shit, I'm gonna harm the children"—forced me, begrudgingly at first and voraciously at the end, to pursue an odyssey of truth. Not merely a truth aimed at vindicating me against the specific charge that had landed me in the mental ward, but a truth demanding I double back and sift through the remnants of my life before that fateful Thursday night.

CHAPTER 3

CROSSING THE EMOTIONAL RUBICON

"A strong man acts within that which constrains him."

I woke the next morning of March 6, 2015, after mere labored minutes of sleep, ragged and with one thing on my mind: springing myself from this toxic swamp.

The day started with a meeting with Dr. Wong, the stand-in psychiatrist for the weekend. He informed me—in the first dilemma in a series of ludicrous Catch-22-like quandaries—that I would be in the hospital at least through the weekend because the regular doctor didn't come on Fridays due to budget cuts. I squinted as I tried to wrap my admittedly fatigued mind around the notion—fiscal shortfalls and reduced staff meant not a shorter stay, but a longer one. If I had read Orwell when assigned to do so in school, it might not have come as quite a shock. But, alas, my general indifference to academics caught up to me, and I thought, *You're seriously telling me I'm stuck here for the weekend because the appropriations committee in Sacramento was unduly parsimonious on mental health funding?*

And so, the tone was set, and I found myself a prisoner on the vertiginous Del Amo roller coaster. At least there were visiting hours that night, and I could talk with Dana, get updates on the boys, and get back to my life, even if it was never going to be quite the same again.

Until then, however, there was protocol to maintain. There were group therapy sessions, and while optional, I was sure they would ground me and give me a sense of normalcy to stave off the chaos. I tried to be helpful and participated as much as I could. I lingered after the session to chat with a couple of patients, and my conviction that I did not need to be in the hospital was only strengthened by the interactions. The day dragged by, and as the visiting hour drew nearer, my excitement grew to a near-euphoric state. Salvation would soon be at the doorstep.

Finally, the doors opened, and the stream of visitors began. My pulse raced like a child on Christmas morning as, one by one, the faces emerged—but Dana's was not among them.

First, bewilderment. Then despondency. Everything I thought I knew to be true about the world suddenly became false. Everything I thought I could rely upon was revealed as illusion. I crumpled into a stained sofa in the common room as visitors bade farewell to the assembled patients.

Then a nurse called my name and told me I had a phone call. Completely emotionally disoriented, I walked to the telephone with visions of atonement and rebuilding my life in mind. But all hope was soon obliterated.

"Have you taken your medication?" It was Dana's voice, but it was frosty and disconnected. No emotional support or inquiries into my wellbeing; no update on the boys; no apologies for some big misunderstanding. Her question was even more baffling because I hadn't been prescribed any medication, nor even had a conversation about it. I told her this and it didn't seem to register. The conversation, in all its perverse civility, compounded my disorientation. It was as if we were speaking different languages. I begged her to tell me what was going on, what diagnosis she thought demanded I take medication, and she responded robotically. "Just take the medication." She betrayed not a sliver of empathy, but rather kept quizzing me on the state of medication I had not been prescribed.

Our emotional universe had become, by this time, a house of cards collapsing on itself. But in that moment of genuine truth between us, I felt a sense of unspeakable betrayal—regardless of the debris that littered the path we'd taken, I could not imagine that she would so coolly allow me to rot in that forsaken place.

After the call, I was fully coherent and in control of my faculties, albeit emotionally exhausted and rather agitated as the horror penetrated: the person who I thought was my umbilical cord to the life I had been hijacked from was not a lifeline after all. The isolation was punishment; I had no phone, no wallet, just the coaster with the baby picture of someone I had known for decades who was fast becoming a stranger.

Later, back on my mortuary slab, I settled in for another anxious night. My bedroom at home was a sanctuary, with expensive sheets and pillows, a place where I could rest if not sleep. The canaries gathering were growing into an aria, a name with such a regal ring. Nothing before me was now painted with such transcendent glory. There, in that pen of mentally ill people, I only felt the canaries shaking and choking in soot, struggling for air. I was vulnerable, and the child in me recognized this nocturnal anxiety.

Sleep has eluded me my entire life. I think of sleep as an emotional church, and I've longed for its salvation. Humans need sleep so desperately to be at our best. Yet, even as a child, it always evaded my grasp.

I was ten years old when I started sleeping with a kitchen knife under my pillow. I would secretly return it to the cutlery drawer each morning. The combination of my mother's volatile temper and my father's apathy made me reach for the curious symbol of safety so that I might get some sleep.

As a young boy, I wet the bed almost nightly. I would dream I was awake and standing over the toilet, only to wake up drenched. I had no cuddly toy to comfort me at bedtime and, forced to improvise, I pretended my pillow was my imaginary bedfellow. I called it Peter. I would make up bedtime stories and share them with him in whispers to stave off the loneliness and help me sleep. Peter never complained about my nocturnal challenge, even as he became stained and raggedy. My mum tried to throw him away on multiple occasions, but each time I would retrieve him from the rubbish bin, and eventually took to hiding him away each morning.

After a few months of daily soiled sheets, and at her wits' end, my mother brought home a contraption known as a "shock" blanket, an apparent cure-all for bed wetting. It was a plastic blanket that lay on my mattress, connected by red and black cables to a clunky, antiquated contraption that looked like a portable car battery charger. When the blanket detected liquid, a clanging buzzer rang loudly, the blanket vibrated, and I was "shocked" back to consciousness. Sadly, her stab at mothering proved futile because the contraption did not work properly. If I so much as shifted slightly in bed, the alarm would sound, and I would get a jolt. My nightly fears of waking up drenched were then compounded by this newfangled electric sleep disruptor. I would try to lie motionless so as not to set the thing off, but it only heightened my anxiety. After six months of what seemed like death by electric bed, I still woke in a puddle of my own piss, and my mother mercifully gave up on it.

In the blackness of the dismal hole that was the mental hospital, my mind strayed to that distant past and my prior humiliations. But, pressed by more immediate concerns, I waged war on my body, poking and prodding myself to stay awake, determined not to be attacked again. I mused over how circumstantially dependent the benchmarks by which we gauge good fortune truly are. A week before, I would have considered getting a favorable morning tee-time at my country club the height of good luck. Now, merely avoiding a physical assault in the middle of the night was enough for me to say a silent prayer of thanks.

my wife of twenty years. In fact, I realized, any escape plan must be hidden from her. Dana was now the impediment to my freedom.

My survival instinct crystallized during that meeting. I realized I had no one to rely on but myself if I was going to escape that claustrophobic prison. It was a position I had been in before; I had read it in scripts, seen it in movies, in stories where the protagonist knows a deep truth that he just can't get anyone else to believe—like *Cuckoo's Nest*, but devoid of any entertainment, wrung instead with human suffering and loss.

I was going to learn the hard way that, once in the mental healthcare system, even the most innocent and innocuous of comments can be twisted and used to nefarious ends. Insisting you're not crazy only makes you sound crazier.

Suddenly, long-time friends and acquaintances filtered behavior that had previously raised no eyebrows, and came to unfounded conclusions. How easily people become sheep! After all, sane people aren't sent to the psych ward, right? We are all heavily invested in the conceit that our institutions are fair and our systems uncorrupted. Why? Because the alternative is too frightening. Because we don't want to know that you, as easily as I, could be committed to a mental institution based on nothing more than a ten-word lie.

● ● ●

The previous year, with Dana's blessing, I had reached out to start therapeutic sessions with psychologist Dr. Katrina Wood. It was the first tentative acknowledgment that I was in debt to myself, that the wounded child inside me needed repairing. Two days before I was handcuffed, I sat in my office and wrote in my journal:

March 3, 2015—Self Musings

A year ago, I took the difficult step to seek help. It was my first authentic acknowledgment that I had problems that needed fixing. My therapy initially involved understanding what was broken internally. To get to the root of these continuing issues and put an end to the repetitive nature of destructive behavior I first had to dig deep into the dark recesses of my emotional psyche. The very core of my soul. Confronting the abuse I suffered at the hands of my parents was fundamental to this process.

The painful realization that my ethical framework was flawed was at first overwhelming and confusing. I came to understand that I must account for and resolve the inconsistencies within my internal value system. But how? To reconcile emotional trauma and construct a core value system is a deeply immersive and ongoing process. One that does not consist of loyalty to one's subjective whims, but to rational principles.

This is what I have been working on and must now focus on above all else.

It is evident that this search for identity, value and integrity cannot take place under the microscope of community.

It is time to retreat.

Reflect.

Please understand that I do not consider myself the hero of this story. As proven evident by my journal entry, I knew destruction and growth were my own responsibility.

It is true that there are things I did to destroy trust in my marriage. But it is also true that I did not deserve what happened to me in March of 2015. Nor do I deserve, to this day, to crawl through the byzantine maze of the family law system. Most important of all, my sons do not deserve to be denied a loving, perfectly sane and competent father.

During my first call with Dana from Del Amo, I pleaded with her to help by bringing some psychology books recommended by Dr. Wood. Dana denied me—in my state of utter vulnerability—even that small favor.

Dana brought me a copy of Keith Richards's memoir, *Life*, maybe as some sort of unarticulated critique of my worst behavior. Whatever her inexplicable reasons, she also brought a script from my literary agent. And for that I must thank her, because those hundred pages of paper would prove key to getting the hell out of Del Amo for good.

CHAPTER 4

THE LITURGY OF THE COMPROMISED MAN

"Humble yourself or life will do it for you."

Not knowing how you came to be imprisoned makes escape all the more difficult—it is true of our minds and it was true of the cadaverous psych ward in which I was detained.

It was March 9, and there I was, stranded. The movie *Castaway* came to mind—Tom Hanks stuck on that island, grubbing for twigs and brush to summon a flame. There was some familiarity in my position, because I had understood for a long time that, in some fundamental way, I had largely been emotionally stranded for much of my life.

I was the misfit middle child, the filler in the sibling sandwich, forced to grow up in a hurry and make adult decisions long before I actually became one. My childhood was so thoroughly suffused with profound parental dysfunction that I quickly reached a point where I had zero concern over behavior that might compromise my family life. After all, you can't care about destroying something that doesn't exist.

Compounding these problems, I had always possessed a determination to make an impression. My earliest memory is of an impromptu performance at a family wedding in the summer of 1972. I was four years old. The father of the bride had just delivered a long-winded speech, after which the groom cleared his throat and nervously shuffled through his prepared notes for what seemed like an eternity. Somehow, even at that tender age, I sensed a pall had fallen over the proceedings and, seizing the moment, climbed unnoticed atop a table, took one sharp intake of breath, and with preternaturally cocky conviction, broke the uncomfortable silence. "We're only here for the beer!" It brought the house down. Just a small kid, I had gone with my gut, jumped into the breach, and been rewarded with joy. My gut never seemed to fail me, until it did.

This combination of my nature, and an utter lack of nurture, forged a risk-taker. By my mid-teens, I started regarding myself as something of a pathfinder and pioneer. My risk-taking was, for the most part, in service of my willingness to court failure as a means of achieving success.

And so, as the hours ticked by in Del Amo, I came to understand that I would need to rely on my own wits and daring to escape. Isolation holds utility. Solitude can clarify the soul and the objective. Confinement can float like the smoke of a ritual, distilling thought, bringing everything down to the root.

It was time for an escape plan.

• • •

Fate occasionally smiles, even in the bowels of a mental institution. The evening of Day 4 in purgatory, I came across the facility's head nurse and begged her to spare me a few minutes for a private conversation. She obliged and took me to a room adjacent to the hallway. Up to that point, I had been dismissed every time I tried to speak in confidence to a nurse or doctor. And so, stripping away all pretense, I asked her how to get out of the place. For reasons I can't explain but for which I'm eternally grateful, she injected a flash of humanity and grace into Del Amo's otherwise clinical gauntlet of icy detachment and gave me the blueprint for escaping.

She said I had two options. First, I could request a court hearing, where I would plead in front of a judge. I would have to wait a couple of days to get a court date that might be scheduled weeks down the road. Second, I could ask for an immediate proceeding with a hearing officer, one of dozens of vaguely-named title holders in the legal system that—to the ears of complete layman fumbling through the fog in the first few days of a life implosion—are completely indistinguishable from one another. The nurse told me that if it didn't go the way I hoped, I would have no path to appeal and would have to wait even longer to get in front of a judge.

Mr. Risk-taker chose option two.

Despite the stark danger of this path, I had a purpose and was exercising some personal agency within an environment designed to strip me of it. I summoned the energy to survive another night and prepared for my fate.

The following morning, I came face to face with Nadaly, the resident Del Amo social worker, one of the people who could be described as a true enemy. She had arrived with her mind already made up about me, possessed of biases I would only grow to understand later. The first person to interview me was a DCFS caseworker who was charged to draw some objective—or so one would assume—conclusions concerning my health and welfare as a father. Though I only suspected it then, I know now that she was acting in concert with Dana, and that the meeting was nothing more than perfunctory pretext to paper her predetermined—and false—conclusion that I had abused my children.

The day before, I had met with the Del Amo social worker who peppered me with many of the same questions and was cursed with much the same demeanor—cold, standoffish, and disinterested in my questions and my version of events.

In the afternoon, I was summoned to the Star Chamber for a date with the hearing officer who would be the first in a litany of "judges" to decide my fate. I prepared for the hearing and met with my patient advocate. He unfortunately spoke little English, but nonetheless explained that the officer in charge of my hearing, to his knowledge, had never ruled in favor of a man. He followed up that fatalistic fact by explaining I would have very little time to talk. These elements would prove to be standard fare in the coming months.

I slogged into the hearing room and stood before the hearing officer, playing my assigned role in a proceeding that would have made Kafka whistle in amazement. The bizarre ritual proved its fraudulence from the first moments when, from a statement the police had provided, the hearing officer recited:

The patient stated to the police, "I'm sick of this shit, I'm gonna harm the children."

This defamatory falsehood—never more than a malicious allegation about me phoned in to authorities—had now become something I had said *directly to the police*! And just like that, this life-destroying lie, through repetition and distortion, assumed the patina of truth.

The DCFS' partner in crime, the Del Amo social worker, then took her turn and promptly did everything possible to bury me. As she read from a statement, the lie morphed again right in front of my eyes:

"*Someone* called the police and alleged that *someone* heard the patient say, '*I'm sick of this shit, I'm gonna harm the children.*'"

Wait, what? Now someone other than the police had heard me utter these words? Same lie, different form.

Casting a light stone on the altar of fair play, the hearing officer interrupted and demanded to know why there were two versions of the police statements directly at odds with each other. One claimed I had said these words to the police, and another alleged that someone had called the police to tell them they had heard me say them.

The social worker stumbled through a nonsensical apology for the irreconcilable stories, then moved on to her damning report based on opinions and comments made by my wife, my mother-in-law, and Dr. Grossman, whom she claimed was our family care practitioner. I explained that he was not our family doctor but simply a parent at my children's school and a member of my golf club.

And here the Catch-22 cast its net yet again. It goes like this:

Your freedom is ripped from you. Your whole world is cuffed and stuffed, and you're reeling from the most profound betrayal in your adult life based on fabricated and hearsay evidence. And, because you're human, you get a little agitated. The social workers jot down your agitation in their notes, sprinkling it with a hint of malevolence. Your wife and her mother and some doctor falsely claiming to be your family caregiver say that you "don't quite seem yourself." And that's it—that's enough to keep you institutionalized and paint you as a danger to your own children.

Ask yourself, *Would you feel like yourself in these conditions?*

In the end, the Del Amo politburo would have its way. Something as prosaic as the truth mattered little in that hearing room. The hearing officer, despite being obviously troubled by the inconsistent statements and admitting the "evidence" had tilted toward springing me, would not authorize my release. Rather, she encouraged me to take the matter up with a judge whom she was convinced would allow me to leave the facility.

To the untrained ear, this sounds a lot like, "It seems like you're innocent, but I'm not going to do anything about it." To the untrained eye, the social worker and DCFS officer plainly saw their jobs as preventing my release despite any evidence to the contrary. Everything I've learned in the years since has led me to believe that untrained ears and eyes are to be trusted, because they're also untainted by the gunk muddying up a corrupted system where most people make their decisions based on gross gender biases and a self-serving instinct to cover their own arses by kicking decisions down the line.

I then experienced a lone heart-warming moment as I exited the hearing room. I was met by a group of fellow patients who wanted to know the outcome of the hearing. They had all donated coins for me to make a phone call, and Alexa, a meth addict, delivered the quarry. I was grateful for the support, yet understood that when a meth addict delivering a handful of quarters and dimes is what passes for salvation, you know your life has taken a steep turn south.

Then arrived a slice of actual salvation. Through the glass window, back in the hearing room, I noticed a heated discussion between the social worker and the hearing officer. The social worker stormed out, marched over to me, and unhappily exclaimed, "If you are able to confirm you have a place to stay, we may let you out tomorrow, although you'll have to see Dr. Sharma tomorrow afternoon when he makes his rounds for the final determination of your release protocols."

With a glimmer of hope, I hastily attempted to make sense of this twist of fate. If I could confirm I had somewhere to stay, I *might* be released from the psych ward the following day? My mind raced. I remembered that Patrick Fabian had said I could stay with him, but the only phone number I had etched in mind was Dana's. If I could remember any number other than hers, then I'd be able to connect with an outside lifeline. To my dismay, I realized I had no other phone numbers committed to memory. Oh, how I longed for the halcyon days before cell phones, that simpler bygone era before device dependency when we actually memorized numbers.

And so, I readied myself for the most important phone call of my life. My conduit to the outside world was the very woman doggedly trying to keep me inside this dystopian hole.

I called Dana and laid my heart out for forty-five minutes straight, begging her to get me out of this place. I was emotional and as vulnerable as I had ever been with her. It was a searing conversation, at least on my end. She was mostly silent, and ended with, "Greg, take your medication." Then she hung up.

Patrick called a short time later and rescinded his offer of help, giving no reason. A bloody one-two punch. Our friendship ended at that moment.

I drifted back to my bunk and lay there, physically and emotionally paralyzed. I realized that it was in no way an exaggeration to call it a coup, an ouster conceived in deceit, launched swiftly and with military efficiency with no regard for the collateral damage, with the express goal of displacing me from my life.

I tried to pull a phone number from my mind—any old friend, acquaintance, collaborator. Nothing came. Had I really run out of options? Did I have any uncompromised friends left?

Then fate intervened, catalyzing an unexpected tumble of moments. I felt a pestering itch on my ankle, my foot spilling off the bed and resting on the floor. I labored to summon the energy to scratch it and, as I leaned down, I noticed the script Dana had brought me on the floor. In small type, in the corner of the title page, was the telephone number of my literary agency.

Seven numbers, idling on that page—a lifeline.

I gathered a few more quarters and called the number. It was 8:15 PM, and my well-earned pessimism tried to convince me it was a fool's errand. But, miraculously, one of my agent's assistants answered the phone. I was momentarily overwhelmed by the stroke of luck and the voice beyond the fence. I gathered myself and quickly explained the situation, trying to punctuate my words with appropriate dramatic weight to ensure that he appreciated the seriousness of my dilemma. It was profoundly important, I explained, that he take my password and access my contact list on iCloud.

Within moments, I had the phone number of Dr. Wood and my manager. Pressing on, I wheeled through my mental Rolodex, scribbling furiously on a tattered piece of paper the names and numbers of anyone and everyone who came to mind. I called Jay, my agent, and discovered that Dana had left no stone unturned. She had completely carpet-bombed my career, calling him, the kids' school, and others to explain that I was institutionalized and dangerous, incapable of handling or receiving work; that I should not be sent on any new jobs, and my career should be considered on hold.

As I attempted to keep my legs from buckling at this news and labored to explain yet again that, no, I wasn't insane, the other pay phone rang. I answered it to Dr. Wood's voice on the other line. In a scene that would not have made it through editing in an *I Love Lucy* episode, I held a phone in each hand, conducting two conversations simultaneously through different receivers, monopolizing the conduit to the world beyond the Del Amo gate. I might not have been crazy, but the circumstances were undeniably insane.

I told Jay to call me back, blocking anyone else's use of the pay phones. I had a brief conversation with Dr. Wood, and then called my neighbor, Brian Jackson, and secured a spot on his couch. Finally, a confirmed place to stay!

Brian, when asked, said of course I could stay at his house when I was discharged. He said his kitchen door would be unlocked and gave me the key code to his garage, which I scribbled down hastily. The temporary refuge was only five hundred yards from home. I thanked Brian and hung up to call Dr. Wood back, keeping the other phone line open for Jay.

Dr. Wood was a guardian angel, appalled at what I told her. She promised to have an Uber pick me up and bring me to her office if I got out the following day. Our conversation, filled with trauma and tragedy, was accentuated with morbid comedy as we came to realize that, while a world-class wonder at psychiatric treatment, she had no idea how to call an Uber. I had to walk her through the logistics of the smartphone app. Then, after another quick call with Jay, I shuffled back to my bunk and crashed into a deep, exhausted sleep.

. . .

The next day unspooled like the others, starting with a group session. I could only half-listen to my fellow patients as I looked for Dr. Sharma. Early morning turned late morning turned early afternoon. Finally, Dr. Sharma appeared. I ran to him—he signed my discharge papers, and a massive sense of relief moved through me. I was close, so close. Then the seconds became minutes and the minutes hours as the paperwork was processed. My last order of medical business was to retract the consent forms that allowed Dana and her mother to access any information about me.

Confirming my suspicions that the Del Amo social worker was communicating with Dana, she called and asked if I was about to be released. So tantalizingly close to freedom, I would not let her get in the way. I lied.

At 6:15 PM on March 10, I walked out of Del Amo a fundamentally different man than the one who'd been forced in five days earlier. An hour later, I arrived at Dr. Wood's. She greeted me, soothed me, and listened to my situation. Unbeknownst to me, while I was unpacking the previous six days of psychological torment with Dr. Wood, someone was at the North Hollywood police station bolstering their early advantage, building on the story of their original call to the police and working hard to rebrand me as a menace to society and an abuser of my own children.

I had to decide where to go. Dana had told me I could not legally go home. In my condition, I didn't question this, which perhaps was one of the most fateful decisions of my life. I imagined strolling through the front door and hugging my kids, but didn't want any more conflict to derail my fragile freedom.

And so, Dr. Wood dropped me off at Brian's house. Brian is in the financial services industry, and always told me we were "foxhole guys," which in man-speak means we were friends who would always be there for one another. In truth, it's an ill-fitting metaphor, as the two of us couldn't have less in common with soldiers under enemy attack in a muddy ditch. In truth, we were a couple of pampered, privileged friends from the golf club, both in self-indulgent industries with comparably self-indulgent day jobs.

But worse than his self-aggrandizing rhetoric was the fact that Brian, despite his chest thumping, would turn out to be anything but a foxhole guy. In fact, he, like several others, denied me in my greatest moment of need and scurried for cover while the volleys rained down.

But as Dr. Wood dropped me off just a few meters from my home in the rarefied air of Toluca Lake, I was still floating on the magical feeling of being back in the world, the smell of freedom wafting over me like the invigorating fragrance of freshly cut grass.

CHAPTER 5

PRELUDE TO A TRAVESTY

"Faith and belief can be a most dogged pallbearer."

I walked up the driveway to Brian's front door, my mind racing and heart breaking, trying to get my legs under me and my newfound freedom. It was a freedom not adorned by gold-plated, material accessories, but merely by the value of my own integrity; freedom not defined by false pre-March 5 assumptions, but by free will, by choices to be virtuous or vain, generous or greedy, kind or cruel; freedom to seek redemption.

Brian's was a dozen houses down the street from my own. Having been denied by so many friends, I imagined the collective consciousness of my community had branded me a villain, a menace whose banishment from the tribe was essential to this veritable Stepford, returning to the comfort of the secrets and lies maintaining its pretext of nuclear and communal families. I imagined myself in the middle of a Toluca Lake firing squad, with a red letter painted on my chest.

Brian, for his part, was embedded in the privileges and indulgences of the community. It was Tuesday evening, but he and his friend had been drinking, and they took me inside where their party continued. We spoke for hours, the two of them descending into oblivion as the alcohol consumption continued. Eventually, houseguest or not, I was charged with the herculean feat of hauling a 300-pound ex-football player up a staircase to his room.

In the quiet hours of early morning, the dislocation of being just a few yards from my home and my sleeping children began crowding in on me. At 4 AM, I called Dana from Brian's phone, the use of which he had granted me permission before crashing. The phone may have connected me to Dana electronically, but the emotional gulf was insurmountable. We repeated the pattern of the Del Amo calls, and my pleas for her to extend some empathy were again roundly ignored. I asked her if I could come to the house, and she quickly responded that there was security surrounding the house and I would be arrested if I made any attempt. I begged her to consider therapy with me— to go to the Meadows Treatment Center in Arizona together, where perhaps we could begin addressing and confronting our evident trust issues. I begged, prodded, and pleaded. After nearly an hour, I made the first crack in the iceberg; Dana said she would consider attending the Meadows with me. I was euphoric.

That euphoria instantly died with a pounding on the door. My mind turned to ice, my reptilian brain instantly registering that no knocking at this hour could be good news, but not fully comprehending that it was related to the phone in my hand. I opened the door to the police, and they grabbed me by the arms, pulled me outside, and slapped on the cuffs. Dana had summoned them during our call, keeping me on the phone, stringing me along as the cops moved in to detain me.

How can four LAPD officers just enter someone's private residence? As they woke Brian from his drunken slumber, one of the officers explained that they needed to determine if I was in the house legally. There was a pregnant pause, and Brian, after stumbling, said that while I was there with his consent, he didn't know I had used his phone. Standing in his garden in handcuffs, I stared at him. "Foxhole guys, huh?"

"Kiefer, can we sit down for a moment, please?" I asked.

He looked conflicted. "Have you talked to Dana?" he replied.

"I can't. She has a restraining order. I've been accused of child abuse, and I was locked up for a week. Look, I can explain everything in time. Just, right now, can I sit down?"

"You have to talk to Dana," he repeated coldly. She had already gotten to him, but I knew I could reach him. At least I had to try. He was an old friend, the godfather of my youngest son, Smith. I had always been loyal to him, watched the hangers-on and chancers and Hollywood grifters come and go, and had never forsaken him, yet I was too tired to fight.

"Listen, brother," I pleaded, "I've known you for a long time. Saved you from a few scrapes. Always been there for you no matter what. You've always told me if I needed you, you'd be there. Now, *right now*, is that moment. Please, I just need to sit down."

The obvious inner conflict deepening, his eyes teared up a little. "I can't let you in. You need to talk to Dana."

I felt so deeply and utterly betrayed. He and I had known each other for years, working together for long days and nights on many projects. In my moment of need, he couldn't even offer me a safe harbor for a brief respite.

"Then you are no longer my friend," I stated calmly, turning my back on him and leaving his property.

At the time it seemed a fair and measured response. Over a few vicious days of nothing but shackles and closed doors, it felt like I was going to find a way forward, but black and white decisions had to be made in a fog of gray. I would later come to understand that Kiefer had a tough time that morning, weeping after I left. His ex-wife and Dana were friends, too, and feeling trapped between Dana and the deep blue sea, he chose Dana, and I felt the sting of his decision. Understandable, but even in retrospect I struggle to summon much empathy, for his moral conundrum was incomparable to the road that lay ahead of me. Regrettably, our friendship died that morning.

Back at the Fogelsons', Hillary and Adam gave me an update. Hillary explained, painfully, that Dana—a woman she'd been friends with for years—had essentially written her off the moment it became clear she was prepared to advocate for me. Even so, Hillary and Adam negotiated a modest accommodation—they arranged to get my car back, along with my phone and wallet.

Drew walked to my house and returned with my car while I waited at Adam's house, exchanging pleasantries about the utter absurdity of the situation.

. . .

The sight of my car had never evoked nostalgia, but it did that morning. I had last driven it when the world before March 5 prevailed, and seeing it then on the other side of the Rubicon reminded me of how far I'd traveled—and fallen—in a matter of days. But there was work to do, so I plunked myself into the driver's seat and drove with Drew to City National Bank for some cash. The tellers, whom I knew personally, peered at me with a jaundiced eye as I approached the counter. Upon looking at the balances in the accounts, I realized why; Dana had withdrawn sizeable amounts of cash while I had been incarcerated and there was little left. I withdrew a few hundred dollars, and Drew drove me to a local strip mall on Riverside Drive, parked the car, told me to wait and got out. I was left in a stupor, staring out the window.

I remained in that state of suspended shock when then there was a tap on the passenger side window, and I opened it.

"My name is Kevin Berman," said the man leaning into the car. "You can call me the Facilitator. I'm here to help you. Would you like my help?"

"Er, okay," I replied, somewhat bewildered. At that point, really, what did I have to lose?

I emerged from the car to have breakfast with the self-described Facilitator at The Boston Market in Toluca Lake. Kevin wasted little time, telling me he worked for a friend and had agreed to waive his fee. Quite frankly, I had no idea what he was talking about.

Things got deadly serious and Kevin was all business. He informed me I had only two available options. The first was to employ an attorney and start seeking redress through the courts. It would involve divorce, be a protracted process that would be painful for me, my wife, and my children—which, to put it gently, was the understatement of my adult life—and even then, with a film of dew still obstructing my newfound freedom, it struck me as a decidedly unwelcoming door to open.

The other option, according to the Facilitator, was for me to enter a treatment facility as a way of charting a new history that would show the powers that be—namely, authorities at the DCFS and future judges—that I was proactively taking steps to address the issues that had resulted in my incarceration.

"But what issues are those?" I asked, still not quite grasping that optics—not facts—now governed my fate. Truth was secondary to building a new narrative, the Facilitator patiently explained. Posturing that I was tackling my problems and taking responsibility for my perceived misdeeds was essential to my success now—it made no difference whether I had a substance abuse problem (I did not) or whether a rehab facility offered anything of utility to me (it did not). It mattered only that I *appear* to actively address these still unnamed "issues," in this case by seeking treatment for an affliction I did not have. The unavoidable fact that I struggled with *real* problems for which Dr. Wood was *genuinely* treating me was secondary, the Facilitator made clear, to a good performance as the dutiful father taking the accusations seriously, no matter how baseless I found them.

This was wildly counterintuitive to me, but I was willing to talk it over with Dr. Wood.

I did not want a legal battle with Dana. I just wanted some semblance of my old life and family back. I contacted Dr. Wood and we arranged to meet later in the day to discuss the plan.

First, I had to stop at a recording studio for a voiceover session for the animated series *Transformers: Rescue Bots.* I invited Kevin into the studio and willed myself to perform my professional duties as the voice of Dr. Morocco. Surreal doesn't describe what it was like standing in the booth reading my lines that day—pretending to be a fictional, despotic character on a children's animated show—sleep-deprived and wearing the same clothes I had for over a week as the Facilitator watched on from the control room with the producers and voice director. As emotionally shell-shocked as I was, that moment of loopy levity in the face of the absolute absurdity was a welcome relief.

An hour later, Kevin and I met Dr. Wood to discuss my fate. It was decided that the next day I would fly to Santa Fe, New Mexico and check in to The Life Healing Center to address an as-yet-unidentified "addiction."

The next day, March 12, I woke in a Motel 6 after sleeping decently for the first time in a week. As I prepared to depart Los Angeles for Santa Fe, my mind attempted—and failed—to make sense of everything. I wanted to pick up the pieces, but they were scattered over such an immense field of debris that starting this search-and-recovery phase seemed overwhelming.

Adding insult to injury, it turned out that while I was a thousand miles away attending group meetings and counseling from 7 AM to 5 PM every day with no access to cell phone, internet, or the outside world, Dana was continuing her financial assault. She had acted on the information she received from me in Del Amo, and started cashing checks for large sums from our joint bank account, as well as from my production company account. On top of that, she'd started borrowing huge sums of money from my friends ($45,000 alone from one, and more from others) under the audacious conceit that *I* was the one clearing out our bank accounts and leaving *her* destitute.

March 18 was my final day in Santa Fe. With the help of Dr. Wood, my counselors had devised an in-depth outpatient program back in Los Angeles that consisted of intensive counseling, including couples therapy if Dana agreed. Although I was not an addict in the medical sense of the term, I was floundering and disoriented. I was also struggling with a sense of right and wrong, invested in the rationalizations of my life. For that reason, I enthusiastically agreed to the outpatient plan and was thus discharged from the Life Healing Center, after which I boarded a plane bound for Los Angeles.

During the flight home, my thoughts turned to my boys, Charlie and Smith, just as they had for vast swaths of the last week. The draw to one's children is something that exists beyond reason. Parents wrestle with dark imaginings about all the bad things that can happen to their kids, having grown up on a diet of pulp TV where children are snatched from their parents by monsters of all stripes. But imagination can't prepare you for the scenario where the kidnapper is the person you made them with.

• • •

My father left our family when I was twelve—right at the age a boy is moving into adolescence and needs his father most. He had his reasons. My childhood evenings were routinely punctuated by my mother yelling at him, a steady stream of noise pollution dulled only slightly by the ceiling that separated the living room from the upstairs bedroom I shared with my brother. Often her yelling would pause only to be replaced by screams of agonizing pain. I'd try to elicit my brother's help, hoping he'd go downstairs with me to rescue Mum from whatever physical retaliation she may have been enduring. But I always found him sitting in the corner with his hands wrapped around his knees, rocking back and forth, eyes gazing forward. Sobbing, I would shake him. "Nick, please, we've got to rescue Mum." He would ignore me. I couldn't reach him. He'd checked out, dissociating from the downstairs melodrama, gripped in a psychological freeze.

I would then check on my sister, and usually found her hiding under her bed. Sometimes I would force myself to descend the stairs into the lion's den of conflict. One night my mother heard me creeping downstairs and chased me back to my room, then dragged me from my bed onto the floor, ramming her prized Dutch clog into my midriff, winding me, then berating me for being out of bed so late, before exiting with a slam of the door. I feared my mother's rage and needed my father's protection—but he could hardly defend himself, much less shelter me.

The worst terror came when Mum would storm upstairs and drag us from our beds in the middle of the night.

"Get your shoes on. We're leaving. Now!"

Shaken from sleep, we would be bundled into the purple Ford Cortina, still in our pajamas, my elder brother frozen in his dark pocket of trauma, my younger sister wailing like the young thing she was, me falling into the role of shielding them both as my mother chuffed hard on the filter of the Lambert & Butler dangling from her lips. A constant barrage of rage, shame, and self-pity spewed forth from her gullet in a hateful cacophony. She would drive us around for hours like this, assassinating my father's character—or lack thereof.

One night she was in such a hurry that I hadn't had time to close the car door fully before she sped into the street. I spilled out of the car, slammed onto the tarmac, and tumbled along the unforgiving road. There was the ear-splitting squeal of rubber as a car swerved, narrowly missing me. Cut and bruised, I picked myself up as my mum screamed and jumped back in the car. Instead of an apology, she shamed me to my core: "Make sure you shut the door properly next time." Nothing quite like a mother's love.

This nighttime escape routine became depressingly predictable throughout my childhood and always ended in the same desultory anticlimax—after driving us around in the middle of the night, she would abort the mission to return home and we'd end up back in bed with no explanation as to what had happened or why.

Every time, this brought me to an emotional paradox; I was terrified my mother would leave without me, and equally terrified she'd stay.

I had resolved that this wouldn't be—and wasn't—the case with my beautiful boys. I was certain they would be confused and sad at my disappearance. Of course, we were all once children, growing up with our oversized kid imaginations. But even the most powerful mind can't conjure the enormity of a parent leaving for good. I know the loss is profound and lasting.

And so, I had to make things right—and fast. I had to keep our family together at any cost. Little did I know I was about to make the most serious mistake of the early days of my family disintegration, a decision that demonstrated what little I understood about divorce and the "authorities" within the system, even with all I had been through in the last few days.

• • •

I arrived at my house just before 11 PM. I had entered my home a thousand times as master of my domain, but now I hesitated as my instincts pleaded with me to reconsider. I placed my bag in the driveway and contemplated the least disruptive way to see my boys and talk to Dana about our future. I still believed we had a future, despite all evidence to the contrary, and despite the fact that she had done everything within her power to make it clear she wanted nothing to do with me.

I had tap danced through countless scrapes before, though, and I had always talked myself out of trouble. Surely, I thought, my remaining charms sufficed for one more trip to the well. The rationalizations inevitably followed: *Just let me get away with it this time, God, and I will be righteous forever more*, I convinced myself. Ah, the liturgy of the compromised man.

My delusional, quiet confidence was amplified by a small technical inducement. Dana's restraining order was temporary and had by that time expired. I was all too aware that if I called her on the phone, she would immediately call the police, but I wasn't legally prohibited from entering the property, and I still clung to the prosaic notion that if I could just speak to her, we could find some resolution to this ugliness.

I opted for the direct approach and rang the doorbell. Dana answered the intercom, screaming at me to go away and threatening to call the police. Then she hung up. Red flag—but I would not be deterred.

I went around the back of the house in the dark to a door that was usually left unlocked. Dana's uncle, Dres Mortenson was standing at the door. (I would learn later from Charlie and Smith that Dres had been making physical threats toward them while sleeping in their bunk beds.)

Another red flag I promptly ignored. I proceeded to jostle the door handle, but it would not open.

A man not gripped by monumental personal tragedy and dislocation might have interpreted the overwhelmingly obvious message that Dana did not want me in the house, and would interpret any effort to enter as both provocation and excuse to beckon the police sergeant to make good on the threat to rid the neighborhood of the likes of me. But I was not that man, and I only became more determined to enter. That, unfortunately, entailed the act of breaking and entering into my own home. Unable to wrest the door open manually, I broke a small pane of glass so that I could reach in and open the door. In doing so, I had just ensured I would never set foot in my house again.

The burglar alarm began to wail as I proceeded to make my way up the stairs to the master bedroom. Dana sat on our bed with the phone in her hand. This was it—the moment I'd been planning since March 5. *I'll explain the whole situation to her*, I thought, *and she'll come around as she has so many times before.* I had always been able to predict when the music would stop, and get to her before it was too late. But I couldn't hear a thing over the alarm as I walked into our bedroom.

"We need to talk," I implored. "Please, for the sake of our family, please, just talk to me."

"Get out of my house," she snarled, cold and firm. "I've called the police. They're coming to take you away again."

Strike one.

I turned and headed into my sons' bedroom.

"Dad?!" Charlie was ecstatic to see me. We hugged with all our combined might. I clasped his soft cheeks gently in the palm of my hands and looked deep into his soul. "I love you son. Never forget that."

Smith leapt up from the bottom bunk.

"Dad? DAD!"

I hugged him nearly as tightly as he did me.

"Are you legally allowed to be here?" Charlie asked.

"Is your brain still broken, Daddy?" Smith asked.

Strike two.

I exited the house through the front door and waited for the police. After two minutes they arrived, and I waved for them to pull over. I was about to explain the situation when they grabbed me violently, slammed me into the side of the police car, handcuffed me, and wordlessly stuffed me into the backseat.

Strike three. I was out.

In my exhausted state, after a lifetime with hardly a parking ticket, the idea that a faceless state authority could keep me from my kids was so amorphous and foreign. It's like someone telling you you're forbidden from breathing air because your wife says so. You think to yourself—*this can't be real! If I can just sit down and talk with her, we can pull this all back from the brink.* As for knocking out a tiny pane of glass in my own house, I suspect most parents would walk miles along a path of broken glass to get to their kids. I just wanted to salvage my family and talk to Dana and the boys—a fool's errand, I quickly realized. But I had acted out of desperation, not menace.

That said, this incident is evocative in multiple respects. To start, I must and do accept responsibility for my actions, both throughout my marriage and after. The necessity of owning mistakes is, as I have discovered, essential to living a life of integrity. But, in a lifetime defined by tough judgment calls I would only later learn to appreciate as errors, there are few moments I regret to the core of my being. What I did that night is one of them, not because it was particularly sinister—one must understand how bewildering it is to wrestle with the absurd contradiction that you are still the owner of a home you worked your whole life for but are now legally not allowed to set foot in—but because of the massive consequences it precipitated.

No moment better exemplifies the weight of the psychological endeavor of my early days in the gauntlet of marital dissolution than this one. The isolation and terror that infused me in those initial days inside the beast of family law was inescapable. I was, in that moment, staggering in the wake of not merely the false and anonymous accusation of child abuse, but the reflexive willingness of each artery of the system—from law enforcement to Del Amo—to believe that accusation based solely on the fact that the charge had been levied. It was the first, but by no means the last time I found myself confronting a faceless monolith of prejudice and judgment, one that presumed my guilt and condemned me based on that assumption.

None of which is to excuse my conduct. I made a foolish decision and paid the consequences. But the sense of utter and complete inequity of what had transpired nonetheless informed my physical and mental condition and—if I may offer a measure of mitigation on my own behalf—contributed to my misfortune.

My actions meant hours in solitary confinement in a police cell before a prompt return to a mental facility. Even worse, it meant I was about to be thrust into a legal system I had only vaguely heard about. I was to become a fly in a tar pit at the center of a Venn diagram, where the circles of family and criminal law intersected, hemorrhaging emotionally and financially. Harassment awaited me, readied by professionals inside and on the fringes of family law, a Wild West where the foundational precepts on which you thought your life rested are completely inverted.

Naïve and confused, I did not yet know the full magnitude of any of this, but my soul was starting to sense the contours. All I could think of as I was shoved into another police car was that Dana and I were in the midst of profoundly failing our boys, the depths of the failure only coming into full relief many, many months later.

YESTERDAY'S PLAYROOM

There's always room to laugh,
To play,
To live and love.

Always room to roam,
Hide inside,
Reside outside,
Yesterday's playroom.

Sweep the syrupy sweet dusty cobwebs from the vintage toy-chest,
Least invest in,
Lest I still be interested in.

Side by side,
We rode,
Trojan toys,
A past trapped and scrapped,
Piled up pillows dwell nested in gentle pillars, of
Yesterday's Playroom.

The in-appropriations committee walls of political rooms of play,
Crushing constricted constructs,
Of brain crashing waves.
Tarnished,
With moribund murky greyed remembrance
Of stolen hopscotch,
On battlefields of forgotten toy soldiers, in
Yesterday's Playroom.

Storminess shelter,
Of the raging splintered music box in my mind,
Winds me up.

Salad days over,
Tossed up, un-dressed,
Served to re-assess,
Messes left best left,
To reside inside,
Yesterday's Playroom.

CHAPTER 6

DEAD MAN WALKING

"We think change is painful; in reality, pain is changeful."

The back seat of an LAPD cruiser is not where one typically expects to summon the recesses of the mind and draw broad conclusions concerning the state of society. The prospect of incarceration, I can offer with the benefit of experience, evokes a more narrow and personal focus—namely, how to get out of it. Strangely enough, enduring yet another handcuffed journey did get me thinking about something beyond the mere challenge of my current predicament. I could not help but wonder, and articulate to the officers chauffeuring me to my next black carpet appearance: how could this happen in America? How could I, for all my foibles and failures as a husband, be summarily condemned to jail cells, mental institutions and (ill) legal detention, when I had no criminal record, had committed no crime, and had done nothing that warranted such incredibly harsh consequences?

The question gnawed at me then and has consumed me since.

• • •

My experience in the family law system stoked not just anxiety and suffering—though plenty of that—but also curiosity. That is, I was curious how this artifice had been constructed, one that judged me with withering presumptions and yet extended Dana a hall pass as she systematically, and with repeated falsehoods, destroyed my life and career. My subsequent awakening, both intellectually and emotionally, has led me to a conclusion that would have been anathema to me prior to March 5: I believe we are all willing participants in a shameful social kabuki dance, mindlessly fortifying the most destructive false narrative of modern times—that women, just by virtue of being women, are the fairer sex.

I realize this could be a provocation to many. But allow an explanation before settling into judgment on the matter. This fairer sex delusion is, as I have experienced, a painfully misguided distortion of human nature—and we all know it. We need only look to the great literature of the ages to understand that the pedestal we have erected is based on bunkum. In truth, the human condition is much more complex, and breaking bad is an equal-opportunity sport. It takes two to tango.

This is no exoneration of men and our many foibles. It is undeniable, for example, that men are more physically violent. But we have known for centuries there are other verdant avenues for causing our fellow humans pain. We all know that deep in our DNA there are tools at our disposal that can—sometimes quite literally—take another's life without so much as laying a finger on them.

Men and women may exploit these tools differently, yet they share in the capacity to wield them at the expense of others. There is equality in toxicity. The opening narrative of this book does, I hope, convey without ambiguity that, when it comes to divorce with children—when your own flesh and blood and life's work are hanging in the balance—a woman is capable of being every bit as cruel as any man. I don't offer it as criticism or condemnation, but rather a simple, clinical fact that women are human, and thus vulnerable to the occasional malicious frailty in the same manner as their male counterparts.

Just as importantly, a man can and does suffer the resulting torment with the same emotional pitch as a woman. Part of a natural tendency for many men is to be more stoic and less expressive about our suffering. But, despite a growing chorus of people convinced this tendency is a social construction, the truth is more complex, and what many designate with finality as a problem needing to be solved might as easily be viewed as a virtue in many ways.

Whatever one believes, the reality that men feel the pain of family separation is starkly illustrated by what might be the most horrendous statistic in this book. As mentioned in the Prelude, within the regular parameters of the average American life, men kill themselves almost four times more than women, which is a stunning—and largely ignored—tragedy in itself. But even worse is the fact that fathers who have become ensnared in the divorce system kill themselves eight times more than mothers.

Pause and let that sink in for a moment. For every child who loses their mother to suicide during or after divorce, eight children lose their father. This is nothing short of a national health emergency demanding an honest accounting of the conditions driving such despair. We need to ask ourselves: if divorced mothers were killing themselves at eight times the rate of fathers, would we collectively demand anything less than political triage?

The root causes of this carnage are many, and they will be fervently explored. But for our immediate purposes, the critical element is this: our family law system rewards liars. It incentivizes parents—particularly mothers—to bring to the already hideous proceedings the full toxic stew of deceit.

• • •

As I sat in handcuffs in a squad car outside my house, on display for all the neighbors once again, Officer McIntyre talked to Dana in the house. I had tried to explain to him that this was my home, that there was no current restraining order, and that I had committed no crime, but none of that mattered to anyone. I was voiceless and stifled, yet glaringly visible to anyone who could see me in my shackles. To be seen and not heard was to be diminished to a disobedient child. I was at the pinnacle of frustration, yet I could do nothing and say nothing, for if I dared express rage at being made captive in such an unjust manner, I would be labeled as out of control, unstable, or worse—even more of a danger than I was already purported to be.

Dana had another story, a tale almost otherworldly in its miraculous levels of bullshit. She informed the newly assembled law enforcement contingent that I had threatened violence against her and, to heighten the dramatic effect, had telegraphed my intent to kidnap our children. The sheer scope of this mythical plan boggled my mind. I would have had to tiptoe through the house, only to confront Dana in the bedroom—while still planning a kidnapping—before forcibly removing my children as she called the police. A hapless Scooby-Doo villain I might provide the voice for in my day job would have a difficult time stumbling through a more moronic scheme—and yet there was Dana with a straight face, peddling nonsense to the rapt LAPD.

Officer McIntyre, combative from the moment he stepped out of the police car, then drove me to the LAPD's North Hollywood station, where I sat in a solitary cell for five hours. Finally, I was told I was being "detained," not arrested—being detained involves physical restraint and questioning without being charged with a crime, while an arrest is based on an existing charge. Handcuffed in the back of a squad car and then sitting alone in a cell, the distinction wasn't obvious to me. But a certain reality settled in during my third involuntary journey in an LAPD cruiser—namely, that the legal industry traffics heavily in a murky terminology so powerful in its ability to intimidate the civilian and obfuscate the inner workings of an arcane system that it seems like the semantic fog must have been expressly designed to render you lost, vulnerable, and at the mercy of lawyers.

In any event, black-sheeped yet again in my ever-descending Kafka trap coffin, my detention led to yet another evaluation by a doctor and further involuntary confinement, this time to the Charter Oaks mental facility on yet another "5150," which I had by now discovered was an involuntary seventy-two-hour psychiatric commitment. All of which meant more doctors, more evaluations, and another intervention by Dr. Wood to secure my freedom. Rinse and repeat.

I have been told it is almost unheard of to be released early from a 5150 hold (there's big money in making mountains out of mental health molehills). And yet, after only forty-eight hours, the psychiatrists and doctors at Charter Oaks—who could plainly tell I was no threat to myself or anyone else—discharged me. I had, by this time, been handcuffed and detained by law enforcement three times—but mercifully, never arrested.

My release from Charter Oaks followed a similar pattern—like Del Amo, I needed to provide them with an address for my lodging before they could discharge me. My Rolodex lay in a heap of ashes, and I could not bring myself to pull Adam and Hillary any further into my nightmare. Finally, an old friend with whom I hadn't spoken in a decade—who had endured his own horrendous divorce—took pity on me. It was another small salvation.

Some other small, incremental progress was being made. Thanks to Kevin Berman's wrangling with Dana, I managed to retrieve the meager bag of possessions that I'd been forced to abandon in the middle of my driveway when I had been seized and jailed. A man in Kevin's employ eventually arrived to deliver my car.

However, there was a twist, and any sense of grudging return to normalcy quickly died. When I asked for the keys to the car, Kevin's employee presented me with a thick stack of legal papers. It quickly became clear that, unless I agreed to accept this packet—containing a new restraining order—I wasn't getting my car keys or anything else. The Facilitator, having concluded his duties for Adam, was now agitating for someone else—Dana. In movie parlance, my reality had pitched and twisted from *Castaway* through *Intolerable Cruelty* to *The Fugitive* in *The Firm* getting *Gone Girl*-ed with Brian De Palma introducing David Fincher's *The Game*. It was a dark psychological thriller now, and I felt like Michael Douglas's character, trapped in a perverted, sinister reality.

A month earlier I would have told him to bugger off, but I was beaten at this point, and so I snatched the car keys and documents from him and drove away. As I moved along the 210/134 freeway toward my temporary shelter on the outskirts of Toluca Lake, I tried to slow my breathing and enjoy my latest bout of freedom.

After another fitful sleep, I woke in my friend's darkened apartment on Bloomfield Road, the dim light and closed blinds matching my mood. It was my birthday, of all days, and I stared at the ceiling, marveling at the maelstrom of the previous twelve days. I could not, in truth, stand the notion of interacting with anyone. I simply wanted to retreat into myself, and let fate do with me what it would.

I did not have a broken brain, to use the sad words that Dana had driven into our youngest son's vernacular. But I did need help. I thought about the wellness plan that had been developed for me in Santa Fe. I was now free to do the very thing my wife had said she wanted me to do, but which she had actually been actively keeping me from achieving since the beginning of this tragic sequence of events: get help and put protocols in place to prevent things from becoming so distant and defective between us again.

And yet it remained a struggle. I was in dire straits and in denial, still reeling at my role as Dana's co-author in my own demise. As frustrated as I was at Dana for the war she was waging, I still couldn't quite accept the realization that our marriage was over, and I still harbored notions of reconciliation. I refused to accept the demotion on the psychological ladder of my life.

The next day, I received an email from a lawyer Dana had retained which I wasn't completely sure how to interpret. Later, I would find out it was a notice of the dissolution of marriage—that is, Dana's legal notification that she intended to divorce me. It was delivered electronically.

Divorce was a depressing thought under the best of circumstances, but particularly depressing given my nomadic and destitute state. I had just clawed my way out of the second mental institution in a matter of days, and I was already dealing with lawyers.

I was in no way ready for that—few people are. But my mental wherewithal didn't really matter. Divorce won't wait for you to get your life together. The lawyers were gathering at the crest, poised to assume command of the process, and they would not be denied.

Before The Facilitator had flipped and gone to work for Dana, he had told me that, on top of the new restraining order—stemming from the broken glass of my entry into my home—Dana had retained a lawyer and filed for a domestic violence restraining order (DVRO) with a hearing scheduled for early April. Dana had me on my knees, and her lawyer was ready to move in for the kill.

My senses may have been spinning, and I wasn't mentally prepared to confront the byzantine world of lawyers and contested restraining orders—a world that I could only imagine ominously in light of the prior twelve days. But I knew I needed a lawyer. And fast.

The next morning, I had an appointment with Dr. Wood to try and stop the emotional bleeding and move forward toward recovery. Dr. Wood recommended a lawyer named Vicki Greene. I knew nothing about divorce lawyers and trusted Dr. Wood implicitly, so I scheduled a meeting with Vicki for later that day.

• • •

I arrived at Vicki's Century City office—apparently there is an unwritten rule that all Hollywood divorce lawyers must lease office space in Century City or Beverly Hills—and was ushered into what can only be described as a shrine to herself. She occupied a corner office with panoramic views of the Hollywood Hills, the Sunset Strip, and everything in between.

Vicki made her pitch, explaining that she had years of experience and success and that she wanted to represent me. That was all I needed at the time—someone to help. I hired Vicki on the spot. There was, however, one small issue; she demanded a retainer of

$30,000. I almost passed out. The advance fee proved something of a challenge, given that I had been stripped of virtually everything I had and Dana had appropriated all our collective assets. Desperate, I borrowed money from a few remaining friends, any amount anyone could offer to ease my pain: Hollywood divorce, Hollywood prices.

Later that day, I lay in a fetal position on the floor of the dark apartment on Bloomfield Road, crying like a baby in the face of the divorce machinery. The phone rang; it was Vicki. Without so much as a greeting, she barked, "She got Bogen. She filed first."

She delivered these words with what seemed like giddy excitement. Both sentences were meaningless to me, of course, and I struggled to comprehend what Vicki expected me to understand from her proclamation. Apparently, Vicki had a history with Judy Bogen, the lawyer Dana had hired, and believed she could beat her, though, she explained, Judy's involvement ensured a bumpy ride.

Bumpy ride? What I did not know then was that these two high-priced divorce attorneys had clashed in prior courtroom encounters.

Vicki and Judy had represented Alec Baldwin and Kim Basinger, respectively, and that experience, it seemed, had not drawn them any closer.

However, at that moment, I was more interested in the second mysterious sentence and the significance of, "She filed first." Oh, the questions of the naïve. The significance is beyond description. This was to be the beginning of my agonizing education in family law, American-style.

pe·ti·tion·er: A person who gathers signatures for psychological conditioning initiatives to present to an authority for a particular cause.

In family law, the person who files for marriage dissolution is known as the petitioner, which is the equivalent of a plaintiff. The petitioner places themselves at a supreme advantage, and a mother petitioner claiming victimhood at the hands of a bad man is almost untouchable. In family law, much like in many areas of modern Western life, victimhood has become a powerful currency, and the parent willing to communicate their victimhood quickest and loudest gains a massive, sustaining advantage.

re·spond·ent: A person who is called upon to issue a response to a communication made by a petitioner. The term is used in legal contexts and in psychological conditioning.

By definition, if the mother is the petitioner, the father becomes the Respondent—the equivalent of the defendant. The Respondent is immediately at risk of being cast as the de facto villain of the piece, continually burdened with disproving the blizzard of allegations leveled against him—regardless of their truthfulness—and proving they are supremely contrite, praying for the mercy of the court, and working tirelessly to reform their defective character. Always? No, of course not. But the rot in the system means the innocent man is left susceptible to an instant assumption of guilt.

It is not an exaggeration to call the divorce industry an anarchic, untamed cesspool. The constructed artifice ensures a lack of accountability for the professionals who work within its ranks and, in many cases, constitutes a clear conflict of interest.

The cracks in the broken system are veritable chasms for unscrupulous parents looking to expediently debilitate their soon-to-be exes. For reasons I will explore, modern mothers are simply a faster draw and fathers almost always wind-up eating dust as the Respondent. This is not anecdotal rambling. Studies show that educated mothers file for divorce 90 percent of the time[1]. That

---

1   Michael J. Rosenfeld, "Who wants the Breakup? Gender and Breakup in Heterosexual Couples," in *Social Networks and the Life Course: Integrating the Development of Human Lives and Social Relational Networks*, ed. Duane F. Alwin, Diane Felmlee and Derek Kreager (Springer International Publishing, 2018), 221-43 http://web.stanford.edu/~mrosenfe/Rosenfeld_gender_of_breakup.pdf

would berate me for my abysmal performance, like she was David O. Russell going at Lily Tomlin in that infamous behind-the-scenes *I Heart Huckabees* clip. At one point, she accused me of losing the trial for her. (Good to know I was at her service.)

Vicki's manner with Judy was no better. The two would almost snarl at each other simply in passing. In that cage match, I was left feeling like no more than a misplaced prop, a forgotten Starbucks cup left in a shot of a dystopian period piece for a bad bit of continuity. It might have been tolerable if Judy wasn't so obviously getting the better of Vicki throughout the trial, getting inside her head, taunting expertly as Vicki took the bait and lost her cool.

Vicki's focus on confronting Judy was, alas, merely ancillary to the punitive chapter of the trial—the steady stream of friends and professional acquaintances who lined up to testify. How surreal to watch them report for duty. I would sit up with hope as each took the stand. But each was riled up and batted about in the onslaught of Judy's spirited examination, each expertly led by her emotional pitch to relocate past experiences within the new narrative she spun, recasting the benign as nefarious, the innocuous as menacing.

I asked my talent agent at the time, Jay Cohen, to testify, and he made a noble appearance. I had hoped he would be a positive counterpoint to the prevailing winds. He recounted that Dana had called him twice during the week after I had been incarcerated. On both occasions, he testified, Dana had ranted about how I was "psychotic, bipolar, and not fit to audition or work," and had implored him to "tell everybody at the agency to stop working with me." Two weeks after Dana had made those disturbing calls to Gersh, I was dropped as a client, and my livelihood vanished.

The headmaster of my sons' school, Reverend Julian Bull, appeared and took a swing. In another display of emotional alchemy, the banal turned beastly. He proceeded to explain that I had accused one of Charlie's classmates of sexual abuse. The truth was that Charlie had been bullied at school and had come home one day to tell me that his classmate had grabbed and squeezed his testicles. I had merely followed school guidelines, called the boy's father, and invited him and his son to sit with Charlie and me to talk it through. Now I was being tagged as the troublemaker by the Reverend, a man who had always called me his "mate" and had been happy to take my five-figure donations as a matter of course.

The DCFS posse soon took its turn. The social worker who had been instrumental in keeping me in Del Amo—the one from the Los Angeles Department of Children and Family Services—took the stand and had a go at me, smirking as she passed in the court corridor before testifying. She recounted how she had completed her investigation and concluded how substantive her accusation of child abuse against me was. Then she said that I had missed the fourteen-day deadline to appeal the ruling. Upon cross-examination, she was forced to admit that she'd sent my appeal letter, along with the DCFS findings, to my home—the very residence she knew quite well I was legally restrained from setting foot inside. And no, Dana's to-do list did not include forwarding my mail.

Patrick Fabian also had a role in keeping me locked up in Del Amo. Before the madness, I had considered him a friend for years. No longer. He had written a damning declaration about my disposition leading up to March 5 that contained more Catch-22 lunacy. He stated that I had behaved strangely because I *hadn't* become upset when the police came to my home that fateful night. Apparently, he saw my calm compliance as strange behavior.

"Why didn't you protest more, or express anger and outrage at what was going on?" he asked, as if doing so would have improved my chances of being perceived as innocent.

Even Brian "Foxhole" Jackson testified. His brilliant contribution was claiming that he thought I might have a gun in my pocket when I stayed at his home. Isn't that speculation, Vicki? Even I knew that, and yet his ridiculous—and false—testimony was elicited without any sustained objection.

It went on in the same manner for days. Judy railed, Vicki wailed, I flailed. Former friends turned into hostile witnesses and drove nail after nail into my coffin. The Los Angeles Superior Court proceedings became another incarcerating experience as each erstwhile friend condemned me and serviced the foregone conclusion of a guilty verdict.

A fleeting bright spot dawned when Adam Fogelson took the stand. He brushed Judy's contempt aside and clearly and confidently defended my love for my children. Even Judge Kaufman noted the impression he made on her.

But it wasn't enough—not even close, really. Judge Kaufman's reached her verdict: guilty. Of domestic violence.

Kaufman granted Dana full legal and physical custody of our sons and imposed a one-year restraining order, whereby I was allowed visitations three times a week, supervised by a visitation monitor of Dana's choosing.

In issuing this soul-crushing verdict, the judge allowed that a single sliver of light be directed at me. She instructed that if all my drug tests were negative for the ensuing three months, the mandatory drug tests would be lifted, the restraining order would be subject to removal, and the prospect of joint legal and physical custody would open to discussion. As I scanned the rubble of my life in that harrowing courtroom, this single blade of grass became a "golden ticket" in my battered mind. Just stick to the tests for three short months and the gateway to redemption would await. The trial had been a catastrophe, with this as the sole resolution I could take from it.

Now it was over, just like that. The debilitating losses were becoming unbearable.

Later, I sat in the hallway, depressed and debilitated. As a creative who utters and writes words for a living, I returned again to those ridiculous ten words. *I'm sick of this shit, I'm gonna harm the children.* It reads like bad writing because it is—no one talks like that, including me.

Even so, there was icy determination in Dana's eyes as she sat while Judy disemboweled me. The exaggerated picture of the monster presented during day after day of brutal invective was the stuff of talented, fertile imaginations worthy of Marvel comics nonsense.

Tell a man his friend could be a better father, and he shrugs. Tell him that friend is a no-good husband, and he raises an eyebrow. But tell him that friend is a child abuser, and he suspects him forever—the lie invades the psyche like an incurable virus. His regard for his friend is forever diminished. Suspicions linger like sulfuric miasma.

Shivers deep in my soul told me that I had some karmic accounting ahead of me, a confrontation with a conflagration inside. Who was I, really? What was the truth of what I had done?

I knew I had serious work to do. But, as I absorbed the blow of the trial, lost in vulnerability, standing there officially stripped from my sons, instincts of self-preservation demanded I focus on more urgent issues. I needed to get my arms around the enormity of Dana's smear campaign and conquer my denial if I was to mount a head-on challenge to the power of the emotional chain reaction Dana had unleashed.

Robert Oppenheimer, head of the Manhattan Project and father of the atomic bomb, famously and ominously recited an Indian proverb on the morning of the first test in 1945 as he surveyed the awesome fireball he had created. "I am become death, the destroyer of worlds." Oppenheimer, later accused of Communist sympathies and stripped of his security clearance, knew the destructiveness of the force he had authored.

Dana had become the relational Oppenheimer of our family, the destroyer of our world—less the desultory self-awareness Oppenheimer later exhibited. She unleashed forces she did not understand and could not possibly harness. She split the emotional atom, and the resulting chain reaction unleashed a mushroom cloud that engulfed our family. She succeeded in destroying my world, but I'm dubious that she understands that hers and the boys' went with it.

Indeed, the irony is both cruel and rich. Dana launched a scathing campaign, infused with discipline and singular purpose, and the conditions of the legal battlefield undoubtedly favored her, her mother, and her attorney. She consequently won the legal battles, virtually without exception. But she is destined to lose the emotional war because she employed a clinical, legal paradigm on an emotional event, which is predicated at its core on human frailty and redemption. In my view, she had little of the former and not much—if any—of the latter.

Dana used to be the conformist, the cautious incrementalist. I was the confrontationist, the risk taker, the absolutist.

On March 5, 2015, we reversed roles. Dana became the absolutist. Determined to sever the marriage with such ferocity that she could never consider reconciliation, trying to shelter herself from her own demons, her greatest fear was that her will would weaken, and she would let me back in. I, in turn, became the incrementalist, wanting to rebuild and move towards reconciliation.

She was having none of it.

CHAPTER 8

OF SAVAGES AND SCAPEGOATS

"I am not who you think I am. You are who you think I am."

rep·u·ta·tion sav·age: A person who attempts to psychologically recondition the beliefs or opinions about someone else.

Hell hath no fury like a woman scorned, a commonly held truth, one that in normal circumstances elicits knowing laughs and nods, acknowledging that women can be as cruel, vindictive, and destructive as any man without as much as a raised voice, let alone a raised finger. Yet, when a man is struck down by false allegations and is in great need of help, how many look down at their feet and shuffle backward toward the tiresome antiseptic delusion that all men are toxic, and we must reflexively #believewomen?

I have come to believe, based on hard experience, that as a society we embrace the false notion that women are naturally imbued with a more coherent, virtuous moral code than men. I am living proof that this just isn't the case. My life has been negatively impacted by feminine rage, shame, vengeance, and dysfunction, and the fact that society conditions us to keep tales of female toxicity to ourselves does not change that. That basic reality does not make me a misogynist any more than a woman who has been wronged by a string of bad men makes her a misandrist. But it emphasizes a broader truth—we are all human, and women are equal slaves to their passions as men. Beyond that, women's passions can manifest themselves in destructive and ugly ways, occasionally at the expense of their male partners. That is not to dismiss or discount the plight women have endured battling for equality in what has been a male-dominated world, but is only to humbly offer my observation and experience that the fairer sex holds no monopoly on virtue.

Relationship breakups, separations, and especially divorces are predicated by the reputation savage—to regain the perception of loss of face, self-image, and recognition at any cost.

The tattered remnants of my existence in the wake of the DVRO trial and Dana's ruthless assault stand as Exhibit A to that seemingly obvious reality. Feeling like I was at that point occupying my own corpse, I dragged myself out of Judge Kaufman's courtroom and began aimlessly roaming the hall after the verdict, despairing and despondent. Patrick Fabian and I crossed paths, and I stopped him and asked, "Why? Why would you write a declaration against me in the biggest battle of my life that results in me losing my sons and the most important role of my life—father?"

"I only did what I thought would help you," he replied.

I think he genuinely believed it. But the truth was that Patrick was a victim in this, too, as were Kiefer and many others who swirled around my imploding family, caught in the toxic gravity of our family's little black hole.

As ancillary victims of the smear, friends and acquaintances did not have nearly as much control and objectivity over their own words and deeds as they might have thought. Of the litany of people conscripted into participation at my show trial, I wondered how many stopped to realize how little of the comically nefarious result was based on behavior they had actually witnessed me engage in firsthand? Without direct knowledge or empirical evidence, we are all just propaganda peddlers, trafficking in hearsay, rumor, and innuendo.

This crusade of slander was particularly dangerous for me, because Hollywood is a small town, and the smearing of my reputation was not confined to the courtroom. It permeated my entire life, spreading like a virus hungry for victims. Numerous studio executives, agents, managers, and casting directors were parents at my boys' school, members of the country club, or residents of Toluca Lake—and some all three. Dana armed them all with a blizzard of defamations at my expense. The reputation savage made quick work of me.

Not long before our separation, I had reached a personal milestone that represented one more step toward the pinnacle of my profession. I had joined The Gersh Agency. I had been signed by Jay Cohen and had made great strides with his partnership in my writing and acting projects, including producing two projects with Sharon Stone, and a Michael Douglas movie I was attached to direct.

Dana rendered me radioactive to Jay and the entire Gersh agency with just a few phone calls, making unfounded accusations as fact and unnecessarily airing details of our dirty laundry that had nothing to do with my professionalism. I am sure Jay—the man, my friend—was not swayed. But in a town where caution dictates that unfounded fiction be regarded as fact, Jay, as an agent, did what he had to do, and Gersh dropped me. Just like that, Dana cut my career at its knees.

Other schemes of Dana's were more intricate and underhanded. Remember Kevin Berman, the Facilitator who helped me in the days after Del Amo? I came to learn that—while Adam Fogelson had previous dealings with him and urged Berman to keep an open mind about me—he was being paid by Dana's mother's boyfriend, Ira. Berman was a retired LAPD detective with connections to powerful individuals in Hollywood, and, I was informed by a colleague of Kevin's, Dana managed to enlist him to pull the necessary strings to get a police case

PART TWO

LOATHING

Beware the person who stabs you and then
tells the world they're the one who's bleeding.

Beware the Reputation Savage.

The gossip mongers. The sheeple.

And brace yourself to be called a Scapegoat.
A hater of sheep, should you wish to call out
the Wolves beneath the Wool.

CHAPTER 9

BOYS BECOME #MENTOO

"Celebrate, don't castigate, our fathers and sons."

My impulse, as Dana piled up victories in court, was to fight harder—for my boys and for myself. Everything beyond my sons was, and is, in the periphery, a blur out of the corner of my eye. But the cold reality is that the continuous losses in court were feeding a rage against the machine that distorted the purpose of my nearly single-minded focus on the case. I loved my boys and was surely staggering to my feet for them after every knockdown. And yet I also wanted to best Dana, just once—and cleanly—to show her I wasn't powerless and she hadn't fooled everyone. I wanted Bogen blunted and silenced in humiliation. I wanted that for me, not for the boys.

That is a painful concession, though a necessary one. I cannot dispute that some of my motivation was personal, and it would be pointless to suggest otherwise.

However, that is not to diminish the indescribable living-grief and inescapable trauma of being separated from my boys. Most parents understand the profound emotional sustenance their children supply. My love for them, my need to be a part of their lives, and my quest to serve as a role model for them has tempered my self-destructive state of mind in the days and months since this endless family dissolution began. I have often wanted to surrender, my will frayed and ready to unravel. But I don't want the boys to be denied their father, as I was in my youth, and I don't want to become my own father, who surrendered and, in the process, relinquished to my mother the reins of my childhood. I don't have much fight left in me, but what I have left I reserve for my boys.

Summoning that strength, limited though it is, keeps getting harder. As I write this, I am in COVID-19 quarantine; the world has ground to a halt as the specter of an invisible pathogen hangs over everyone. I have been thinking of the hundreds of thousands of divorced parents just like me who already know this isolation, who have been forced into quarantine of sorts by the state. How many fathers already understand, with every cell of their being, how it feels to have freedom ripped away, to suddenly be in a purgatory where you can't hug and cherish the ones who mean everything to you? My boys are half of me—and they are out there, having been hidden away from me behind lock and key since long before any global pandemic.

I can smell them. Sense them. Feel their hot breath on my ears as they fall asleep. Can they still feel me?

It is a soul-crushing reality that I cannot know the answer to that question. Charlie and Smith have been taken from their father, and yet they can never really be extricated from who I am. Indeed, I worry for them, as does any father for his children. How can they be expected to grow into healthy men without their father guiding them? And how will they develop durable relationships with women if Dana, in all her spent rage, serves as their principal female role model? There are myriad forces at work driving the sexes apart, and I am concerned about the consequences of those divisions on our society at large. But I am, and have been for over half a decade, terrified for my boys.

The Gender War and Toxic Masculinity

This, of course, begs an obvious question—what is it to be a man? It is a tricky business nowadays. And fatherhood is even trickier. Don't believe me? Ask a hundred women to read the last two sentences and blurt out the first thing that comes to mind. How many do you think would receive the information without some reflexive thought like, "Oh yeah? You should try being a woman and a mother!"

This reactivity needs to stop. It needn't be a zero-sum game, but we must acknowledge that such ideological gender division undeniably constitutes a war of absolutism, one that must give way if we are ever going to have a chance at both sides waving a white flag. I mentioned this dynamic to a friend recently, who dismissed it. He said there isn't a war between genders, there are just people doing the best they can. I disagree; I believe that is a comforting vision of a place at which I hope we can arrive, but it is simply not where we are, and a trip through family law makes that abundantly clear.

It is in no way hyperbolic to say that American society, and the Western world as a whole, is in the grips of a culture war. The seismic societal rumblings under our feet are knocking us off balance. It seems that no matter the issue, the surrounding rhetoric and debate has a shrill tenor and overwrought intensity unprecedented in recent decades. Whether it's the #MeToo movement, Trump, racism, mass violence, immigration, or so many other concerns, there is a growing chasm between opposing sides, and if you dare express opinions that conflict with a given prevailing orthodoxy, you may be subject to ridicule and personal invective. Daily we hear stories of those just out of step with the mob, finding themselves canceled and discarded, losing friends and often their livelihoods as well.

While it's true that the most vicious skirmishes involve soldiers on the battlefields of social media and cable TV, fear and frustration hang in the air like spent gunpowder, permeating all of our lives, whether we realize it or not. Everyone breathes in the acridity—truck drivers, nurses, CEOs, comedians. It's political, it's social, it's familial, it's personal.

The ascendancy of women breaking through the last of centuries-old barriers to true equality is a beautiful thing to experience. Almost all the men I know look on with pride and amazement at the successful, striving mothers and daughters in their lives, and understand that the #MeToo movement constitutes a long overdue reckoning for bad men.

But why is it that we seem incapable of clearing the runway for women to take off and fly without simultaneously feeling we must ground men? Why must success for one be accompanied by defeat for the other? Why the insistence on the zero-sum game fallacy?

This dichotomy is not an abstraction, but a real and compelling challenge as society navigates the rise of feminism. These huge changes for women are not happening in a vacuum, but rather alongside a necessary recalibration of masculinity—these are two sides of the same coin. It seems to me that the laudable, original objective of the feminist movement that existed to urge us to improve upon traditional manhood and update our operating system has, in certain circles, warped into an all-out assault on everything masculine and a stripping away of any empathy for modern boys—your boys and my boys—who are, and will be, asked to carry a burden every bit as heavy as young women.

When some feminists and feminist allies shout down half of the population, insisting men "sit this one out," I say, "No way! To the contrary." I do not think there has been a moment in my lifetime when it's more important for both men and women to participate passionately in the discussion on how to make things better.

I believe we need to ask ourselves "Where is the empathy for men?" Not in disregard of women's historical suffering, or to discount the scourge of male predation, but rather as a simple acknowledgment that most men are neither predators nor abusers, and that all need and deserve the same empathy and sympathy that women rightfully demand.

The media's response to the unprecedented COVID-19 pandemic is instructive. As I write this, dozens of articles burning through social media opine about how women are the true victims of COVID-19, even as 60 percent to 70 percent of the plague's victims are men. Up to seven out of ten of the people dying behind glass partitions without their loved ones are men, and that fact does not amount to as much as a speed bump in the compulsive drive to victimhood. Instead, barely a month into a global health crisis, there is a rush of articles endeavoring to position women as the true victims of the crisis, loaded up as they allegedly are with more parenting, housework, "emotional labor," and fighting on the front lines in greater numbers as doctors, nurses, waitstaff, and maids. But where is the mention of the predominantly male truck drivers, EMT, police, power grid, and sanitation workers?

One struggles to find even one article in circulation today that ponders what all those lost men might mean for society, let alone how women might *help* their fathers, brothers, and sons avoid death.

If seven out of ten is not a high enough death rate to prompt journalists to ask these sorts of questions, I ask you, what percentage might sound an alarm? 80 percent? Surely 95 percent? Consider these numbers:

- 68.9 percent of unsheltered homeless are men[2]
- 93 percent of workplace deaths are men[3]
- Men kill themselves 400 percent more than women[4]
- 95 percent of war fatalities are men[5]

2   Meghan Henry et al., *The 2018 Annual Homeless Assessment Report (AHAR) to Congress* (The US Department of Housing and Urban Development, 2018).https:// www.wpr.org/sites/default/files/2018-ahar-part-1-compressed.pdf
3   Niraj Chokshi "Workplace Deaths in 2015 Reached Six-Year High," *New York Times*, December 20, 2016, https://nytimes.com/2016/12/20/us/workplace-deaths-2015.html.
4   "Suicide," National Institute of Mental Health, last updated April, 2019. https://nimh.nih.gov/health/statistics/suicide.shtml.
5   Linda, Rosenstock M.D., M.P.H and Joseph, Stephen M.D., M.P.H., *National Mortality Profile of Active Duty Personnel in the US Armed Forces: 1980-1993* (CDC, 2012). https://cdc.gov/niosh/docs/96-103/pdfs/96-103.pdf?id=10.26616/ NIOSHPUB96103.

The truth is, a callous indifference to male death and suffering and a disconcerting comfort level with male disposability has been society's default position for thousands of years. This baseline mentality exists for a whole host of complicated reasons (in fact, male tendencies—youthful risk-taking, for example—are a likely part of this moral oversight), and getting to the bottom of it is beyond the scope of my expertise.

But I pray we can summon the honesty to acknowledge this truth. If the death toll were reversed, there would be front page stories above the fold, in giant font, shouting about a global gender emergency and demanding nothing less than political triage to fix it immediately.

Instead, the grand narrative that I observe taking hold with all the intensity of COVID-19 is that women are primarily the real victims; that women live at the mercy of a patriarchal, hierarchical society designed and built by men to subjugate them in a rancid broth of toxic masculinity.

Ah, toxic masculinity—that stale but ubiquitous call-out. In the past decade, it has become a household phrase, and identifying and culling the herd of toxic ones among us, a national pastime.

What is toxic masculinity? A moment of misanthropic enlightenment; it is the idea that our modern Western culture is structured such that we are socializing our boys to advance and adopt negative psychological states and behavioral traits that not only have bad consequences for men, but also for women and society. Traditional behaviors that were once believed to be virtuous are, in fact, the opposite, so the story goes.

Boys are apparently encouraged by fathers and mentors to keep their feelings bottled up, to be stoic and not "cry like a baby." This nurturing of damaging, stereotypical male gender roles can often result in emotionally stunted boys, who become toxic men, which in turn leads to all sorts of antisocial behavior and often violence that, of course, affects women most.

The speed with which this concept has achieved the status of cultural gospel cannot be overstated. Perhaps nothing better illustrates this than a study of word usage frequency in *The New York Times* since the 1970s. The term "toxic masculinity" essentially did not exist in the newspapers before its debut in 2015. After that, its prevalence spread like wildfire, appearing in graph form as a slope verging on vertical. The same is true for related terms like "patriarchy" and "male privilege."

A Google search for the term toxic masculinity elicits 8.1 million results. Of those, the following headlines show up on the very first page, all written since 2018: "The Boys Are Not All Right" (*New York Times*), "Toxic Masculinity and the Brokenness of Boyhood" (*The Atlantic*), and "How to Fight Toxic Masculinity" (*Scientific American*).

In 2019, toxic masculinity was encoded further into the Western ethos when the American Psychological Association developed official guidelines for working with men and boys for the first time in its history. The document is discouraging, casting what it considers "traditional" male behavior and norms as problematic—toxic, even— at their core. The guidelines mean well and are intended to address some of the real challenges that men face, including more loneliness and violent behavior than women, but they do so by looking at all male behavior through a profoundly biased, negative lens and presenting theory as established fact. Risk-taking and stoicism, for example, are only viewed from the perspective of the negative results that sometimes come to pass, with the positive and necessary aspects of calculated risk-taking wholly ignored. For instance, the man who "impulsively" jumps into the rushing river to save a child may not later obsess about how he almost drowned, nor did he act instinctively, in the moment, for future applause or accolades. So too, the jury is still out—way out—on whether certain behaviors of masculinity are born of dubious socialization or are the function of natural, hormone-driven biological traits. What confuses the rickety picture even more is that many of the same people championing male disposability and shouting about toxic men on the one hand are, on the other hand, claiming there are no differences between the sexes at all.

The idea that men are fundamentally broken humans who might only redeem themselves if they act more like women is not the mere refuge of the gated community of elite academia. The notion permeates the nation's mainstream reading lists. Just one example that received a lot of attention in late 2019 was the book *For the Love of Men* by Liz Plank. On the very first page she tells us toxic masculinity is more dangerous than nuclear war, followed by chapter after chapter of dodgy research in which toxic masculinity is essentially defined as any behavior Plank doesn't like.

For what it's worth, I believe that our modern notions of masculinity are archaic, rooted in a stoic machismo misplaced in the modern world that impairs both the emotional health of men and damages the women with whom they become involved. I was infected by that pathological, bygone sense of manhood, and the virus it embodies wreaked immense havoc on my life and relationships—indeed, there could not have been a March 5 without it. I am not, in other words, embracing or defending the patriarchy in which these aging relics of manliness reside. But what I find so objectionable is the movement that assigns all traditional male characteristics as perforce toxic or misanthropic. That mass generalization flippantly resigns all men, and all manhood, to a malicious and cartoonish detention center of social judgment. Chivalry is not dead; it has been assassinated. And somewhere, irony weeps.

The editor of the feminist website *Jezebel* perfectly captures the caricature this way:

> "Over the last decade or so, I've liked to tell anyone who will listen that the biggest problem facing America is the scourge of testosterone poisoning. The thing is, I'm not really joking. And as Liz Plank demonstrates in her extremely timely new book '. . . toxic masculinity threatens the well-being not just of the women and children around them, but men themselves.'"

Men are absorbing this denigration while they are still boys. In all the focus on leveling the playing field for girls, we have forgotten our boys. Schools, predominantly populated by women, have morphed over the past thirty years to cater to the natural behavior of girls, and boy behavior that was just a decade ago considered "boyish"—like being a little more rambunctious—is now considered problematic.

Psychology and child development expert Michael Thompson phrases it this way: "Girl behavior is the gold standard in schools. Boys are treated like defective girls."

Elementary and high school zero-tolerance regimes mean boys account for 70 percent of suspensions from kindergarten through twelfth grade.[6] As a result, grade-school boys lag behind girls in nearly every metric there is. They get lower grades; they win fewer honors. Studies have shown teachers mark girls higher than boys for the exact same work, and when teachers don't know the gender of a student when marking reading tests, boys receive a mark one-third higher than when their gender is known.[7] Many more women graduate high school and college. Sixty percent of college undergraduate degrees are earned by women, 37 percent more women go to graduate school, and 52 percent of doctorates are earned by women.[8] On top of numbers like these, boys are told they're toxic, day in and day out.

My son Smith once told me during a visit (he was eight at the time) that he was a problem child because he had been diagnosed with Attention Deficit Hyperactive Disorder (ADHD). I did not believe for a moment that he was ADHD, or a "problem child," and I was determined

6   Christina Hoff Sommers, "School Has Become Too Hostile to Boys," *Time*, August 19, 2013, https://ideas.time.com/2013/08/19/school-has-become-too-hostile-to-boys.

7   William Stewart, "Teacher stereotyping means higher marks for girls," TES, March 5, 2015, https://tes.com/news/teacher-stereotyping-means-higher-marks-girls-says-oecd.

8   Mark J. Perry, "Women earned majority of doctoral degrees in 2017 for 9th straight year and outnumber men in grad school 137 to 100," *AEI*, October 3, 2018, https://aei.org/carpe-diem/women-earned-majority-of-doctoral-degrees-in-2017-for-9th-straight-year-and-outnumber-men-in-grad-school-137-to-100-2.

to tell him so. I sat him down and told him that he was not, in fact, ADHD, but that he was a naturally energetic, beautiful, and brilliant boy. No, he protested, he was suffering from ADHD. I asked how he knew that, and he explained that Dana had taken him to a psychiatrist who had diagnosed him as such. Adding pharmaceutical injury to emotional insult, that same psychiatrist had apparently prescribed Smith psychotropic drugs.

This was, of all the punishing and mentally debilitating moments of the entire sordid affair, one of the most soul-crushing. Dana, my son's mother, had taken him to a shrink, who breezily diagnosed him with a mental disorder and then peddled him—*an eight-year-old*—powerful narcotics that would alter his nervous system function, result in alterations in his perception, mood, consciousness, cognition, or behavior and almost certainly affect his intellectual and psychological development. I no longer wonder how our national opioid crisis has reached the depths to which it has plunged. The system is predicated on, and motivated by, the ill-conceived diagnosis of children and the subsequent prescription of drugs to them. I pray for our future and struggle not to weep for it.

More personally, this was not simply a statistic to dwell on, or a reminder of the national crisis. This was my son, an eight-year-old struggling with the loss of his father and seeing that father—whom he'd been taught to now fear—only under the supervision of a stranger who fed the pathology engulfing the entire situation. The crisis had come home, and now I wept for both of us, Smith and myself.

As personal as this is, the broader question lingers: why the urge to label my son, and other boys, a "problem" simply because he strayed from the robotic conformity we now expect from young boys? I consider that departure a virtue, but the world today condemns it as a virtually unforgivable vice that must be purged at all costs.

Drug-pushing mothers replacing fathers' disciplined guidance is unfathomable.[9]

Fatherhood in the Crosshairs

If masculinity is being targeted, fatherhood lies in the bulls-eye. As society has rightly broached the institution of family inclusivity, the traditional role of a family patriarch has been severely denigrated. For thirty years, the virtuous and binding thread that fathers have woven into a healthy Western society has been pulled out of the modern tapestry thanks to a consistent drumbeat of modern feminism, pop culture stereotypes, and a broken family law system. As the appreciation of fathers dwindles, fatherlessness has indisputably grown to epidemic proportions that few are willing to admit.

In 1960, 8 percent of children lived in a home with only their biological mother, and in 2016 that number grew to more than 23 percent.[10] According to dozens of official sources, these children are at a greater risk of facing difficulty in their lives according to just about every measurable metric. They are more likely to misuse drugs, experience abuse, or go to prison.[11] They are twice as likely to drop out of high school[12] and much more likely to live in poverty.[13] They

9 "Attention Deficit Hyperactivity Disorder (ADHD)," CDC/National Center for Health Statistics, last reviewed April 20, 2020. https://cdc.gov/nchs/fastats/adhd.htm

10 *The Majority of Children Live With Two Parents*, United States Census Bureau, November 17, 2016. https://census.gov/newsroom/press-releases/2016/cb16-192. html#:~:text=During%20the%201960%2D2016%20period,from%203%20to%204%20percent.

11 "The Proof Is In: Father Absence Harms Children," National Father Initiative, last updated 2020. https://fatherhood.org/father-absence-statistic

12 "The Importance of Dads in an Increasingly Fatherless America," The Heritage Foundation, June 15, 2018. https://heritage.org/marriage-and-family/commentary/the-importance-dads-increasingly-fatherless-america

13 Gretchen Livingston, "The Changing Profile of Unmarried Parents," Pew Research Center, April 25, 2018, https://pewsocialtrends.org/2018/04/25/the-changing-profile-of-unmarried-parents

are seven times more likely to become pregnant as teens.[14] Children who grow up with fathers in the home have stronger cognitive skills, better health, more confidence, and—counter to the story we're fed—more empathy.[15]

But perhaps our ambivalence to the importance of fatherhood is best exemplified by the instruments society has put in place to prevent men from taking on their rightful role or participating in fatherhood in the first place: paternity laws.

Consider this fact: currently, it is an accepted fixture of modern Western society, legal in many US states, for a mother to conceal from a biological father that he is a father at all. A mother can give birth without ever communicating a thing about it. It goes even further; a mother can knowingly or mistakenly drop another man's name onto the birth certificate and, even if a paternity test scientifically overturns the mistake/lie, the biological father cannot reverse this manufactured reality and gain his rightful status as the true father. He has no right to even see a photo of his child—ever.

Most people shrug at this. After all, there could be good reasons; chiefly, safety for the mother in a sliver of situations. Yes, there are exceptions—but this reality of life is a tragedy for eager and would-be fathers, and betrays our callousness and indifference to men, their emotional lives, and biological parenting instincts.

Laws that encourage this sort of matriarchal duplicity exist even as an ever-growing mountain of clear evidence shows that equal time with both parents is, except in extreme cases, the best scenario for kids. Warren Farrell, Ph.D., considered the "intellectual father of the men's rights movement" and whose thirty-year career focuses on the issues facing men and boys that actually began with the women's liberation movement, has written extensively on the importance of

---

14   "The Importance of Dads in an Increasingly Fatherless America," The Heritage Foundation, June 15, 2018, https://heritage.org/marriage-and-family/commentary/the-importance-dads-increasingly-fatherless-america

15   Cathy Young, "Boys, Feminism, and Empathy," Arc Digital, February 1, 2020, https://arcdigital.media/boys-feminism-and-empathy-748cdb9e23b1

fathers. While we might want to believe that mothers and fathers are interchangeable and expendable, research shows that matriarchal and patriarchal approaches to parenting are contrasting, and dad-deprivation can have serious ramifications on boys' childhoods, particularly in the area of playtime.

For example, when a little boy wants to climb a tree to swing and play in the branches, his mother might be concerned with the possible dangers and risks, whereas his father may see it as a necessary adventure, a rite of passage, of boyhood learning. Again, this greater tolerance for (relatively safe) risk-taking by fathers is borne out by decades of research.

Roughhousing is also a vital experience for boys, and dads more naturally navigate this terrain. Roughhousing engenders a sense of empathy to the self and the other, which helps promote friendship and bonding and can stave off isolation and depression, according to Farrell.

On average, fathers are stricter with their boys and less prone to manipulation. "When fathers are more involved with their sons, there tends to be a lot more boundary enforcement, and therefore more postponed gratification, and they tend to become more successful in life, and more proud of themselves," Farrell says.[16] Boys raised predominantly by dads become more purpose-driven and goal-oriented, better able to discern their *needs* from their *wants,* and are less likely to have challenges focusing.

Needless to say, mothers provide good and necessary parenting from another angle. But balanced parenting cannot take place if the father is not present. There has to be a "Spirit Level of the (S)exes" so that boys can become better adjusted, self-actualized, more disciplined young men. As boys become men, the testosterone coursing through their veins is inevitable. When it is channeled poorly, they can become destructive. A father can help guide this growth and turn destructive to constructive.

---

16   Warren Farrell PhD and John Gray Ph.D., *The Boy Crisis* (Dallas: BenBella Books, 2018).

• • •

"Are you being good boys for Mum?" I'd asked my boys during one of my early visits with them in 2015. Smith looked forlorn. "Dad, we need you home. You give good discipline. Mum can't do it." Hearing my eight-year-old son longingly plead for what he knew he needed, what I knew he needed, what Farrell writes of, what I had given Smith for the first eight years of his existence, yet with no meaningful way to provide him (or Charlie) this paternal elixir, was soul destroying. Without their father in the home, I knew my sons' life trajectories were changing immeasurably, and not for the better. Yet there was nothing, absolutely nothing I could do about it except to love and comfort them in what little time we had together.

As you can imagine by now, the depths of my feelings on this subject are rooted in my own experience in the family law system and its many discontents. All the social science means nothing to Dana and the legions of people like her who can game the family system to strip good men of their rights and effectively kidnap their children. After my trial in April of 2015, I had my first meeting with my boys on a Tuesday night a full six weeks after I was dragged out of my home. Nothing upends a man's telemetry during an already excruciatingly isolating experience than not seeing his own flesh and blood. I had no home to call my own, so we arranged to meet at the park where I had coached the boys little league baseball team the year before.

As I walked across the parking lot, I briefly got lost in the atmosphere of the surrounding park—the smell of the grass, the laughter of the children, the crack of a baseball bat—and drifted back to the last time I had been there with my sons. They had been excited about the coming game, and our banter was simple and effortless. How could anyone ever imagine that, months later, my interactions with them would be supervised by a state-enforced third party?

That first meeting was an emotional wrecking ball. Smith instantly and anxiously announced that he and Charlie had been told by Mum not to, under any circumstance, get into a car with me because I might kidnap them. I had barely said hello, and his disturbing statement hit me square in the gut—all in the presence of the visitation monitor, a ghost of a man charged with scrutinizing our every interaction.

Tragically, the children had been put in a position where they were a delivery mechanism. Smith said that they had been told I was sick in the brain and that I was a very bad man. I wanted to reply in kind, but instead offered only silence and stoicism—not only because of the guard watching the proceedings, but because I knew it wasn't right to communicate through the kids. What Smith said next will forever haunt me—"And the other night at bedtime Uncle Dres was lying next to me in my bed and threatened to punch me in the face if I didn't go to sleep." Then Charlie chimed in to support his younger brother's recollection, "Yeah. He did. And I leaned out from the top bunk and told him he couldn't threaten my brother like that, and then he threatened to punch me too!" I was roiling inside. My sons were pleading with me for paternal protection and I was utterly helpless. Smith then looked forlorn. "I told Mom and she didn't believe us. I don't feel safe about Uncle Dres. I think it's child abuse. He's definitely not going to heaven."

It was difficult for me to be silent, as someone who has made a living by talking. But if I had learned anything about family law at this point, it was that my words would be used as weapons, distorted and re-purposed to try to impose greater restrictions on me and my boys.

I hugged the boys tighter than I ever had before, then explained to them that nobody had the right to threaten them and they should speak to their mother about this serious situation again. We then played together as best we could under the circumstances, but it's hard to approximate normalcy with a man shadowing you and a clock in your head, gonging as the minutes pass until you'll have to say goodbye. It felt like we were three ghosts, trying to play but struggling to learn how to grasp objects in the physical world—a struggle that doesn't go away in two or three sessions. It takes years to approach a new normal, and in fact a new normal is impossible.

I didn't deserve this. In the lead-up to the death of my family, there were some real challenges that begged my attention. I was and I am responsible for my mistakes. But Dana, too, had been diagnosed with her own issues, and together we authored our collective demise. The difference is that, while I was forced into the role of the Respondent, she was never forced by any instrument of the state to confront her own addictive behavior patterns. That cross was borne by me alone; I alone had to atone for my sins. It was me alone who had to take hair follicle tests to prove I wasn't on drugs; who had to appear for random drug tests twice a week and urinate in cups in front of strangers; who had to attend group therapy sessions; who had to spend hundreds of thousands of dollars to dig out of a hole and prove I was a good dad. It was me alone, not her—despite trying to do all the state expected of me so that I might keep those sparse but essential sessions with my precious boys—who would soon be denied even those beautiful gems of time after doing nothing more than eating the wrong breakfast snack.

"Living grief is our world suspended by a unique tear. Our sons.
Our bond with them can never be broken, yet the connection is torn."

—Fathers in Absentia

CHAPTER 10

FATHERS IN ABSENTIA

"The unfair agenda of the fairer gender."

In the days following the trial, a friend named Terence Carter mercifully let me stay at his home. For weeks, I spent every moment obsessed with survival, and the process consumed me. Our survival instinct, I discovered, summons focus, consumes, possesses, and, like a parasite, takes over and decides how we expend our energy. So it was for me.

Then I had a day or two to pause. But with Terence at work, the silence of his home—rather than a soothing respite from the chaos that threatened to overwhelm me—proved crushing. My fatherhood eviscerated, the man in me muzzled and bound, the boy inside the man browbeaten, I sat slumped, shivering despite the morning sunshine, in a cold brew of anger, resentment, fear, fragility, and betrayal. The sense of disconnection overtook me; the isolation gained physical weight as it crowded in like a San Francisco fog. I could not get beyond a profound sense of dread and hopelessness.

As always, my thoughts returned to my boys, to the urgent matter of getting to them, and so practical considerations refused to be denied for long. How do I dig myself out of this mess? Where do I start? I realized that I needed to be honest with myself about Dana in order to get a handle on who she was now, to come to terms with how far apart we were and how far she was willing to go. It was profoundly tragic having to reframe, in a veritable instant, my life partner and the mother of my children as my indefatigable enemy.

Two Broken People Trying to Make a Whole

It was a long way from where we started. I met Dana in 1995 in Las Vegas. Maybe fitting, maybe telling, because behind the surface glitz of chrome and neon lies a cold and confused land with a dirty soul.

By the early '90s, I was an established theater actor in London's West End. I was part of the original cast of Cameron Mackintosh's original musical, *Miss Saigon,* and performed for the Queen in several Royal Command performances. I appeared in TV dramas and sitcoms and then signed a record deal in Germany, after which I had moderate success with a couple of singles.

I had also once starred in Andrew Lloyd Webber's *Starlight Express.* In early 1995, the director and choreographer, Arlene Phillips, called me out of the blue, telling me Andrew wanted me to reprise the role of Rusty in a new Las Vegas production. I had long harbored the notion of moving to America—my career was growing, and yet I had a burning desire for even more, and I was restless in the midst of my abundance. I took the leap across the Atlantic to stake my claim in America's modern-day Babylon.

My arrival seemed an auspicious one. I stared in awe at the neon lights of the Las Vegas strip from the comfort of the first-class cabin as the plane circled. A limo drove me past my name in lights outside the Las Vegas Hilton before I checked in to what would be the most raucous, fun-packed year of my life.

One night, a friend from the production introduced me to Dana. She was moving to Vegas for work.

"She's so cool," the friend told me. "You're going to love her."

Dana and I became fast friends, although she made me work hard for her affection. The Casanova in me wanted to unlock her heart, yet it took me months to decipher her code. One night at a "Boogie Nights" event at the Rio Casino, after months of wooing her relentlessly with my brand of self-effacing humor, I gained a foothold. Nine months later, on June 9, 1996, we married on The Strip in The Little Church of the West nestled on Las Vegas Boulevard, right across from the Mandalay Bay resort.

We enjoyed almost two decades together. But unfortunately, this book is not an affirmation of our success. Like many couples, we were two broken people bonded by trauma, trying to meld into one coherent whole. I brought my own pathologies to our union, of course, as did Dana. For years, I tried to perform manhood and fatherhood in a way that would penetrate her shield, but my efforts were generally for naught; she was mostly incapable of emotional intimacy—no hugs, cuddles, proffers of sweet nothings.

There was no galvanic moment when it became clear to me that our marriage was genuinely imperiled. Growing apart from Dana instead happened in a tragic, glacial way—where you are aware that the drift is happening, but you're not able to turn the ship fast enough. By 2015, our relationship had become a husk of detachment and indifference, but not even in my most fevered imaginings could I have known how virulent her resentment had grown, nor how it would finally manifest in an unfathomable atomic bomb of betrayal and vengeance.

The Dogged Clinging to Gender Myths

Dana and I had, it is now clear, emotionally separated long before she ensured my physical disconnection from her, the boys, and my life itself on March 5. I knew we had reached a crossroads, even in my state of arrested emotional development. I had sent her a text the day before expressing that we were ships passing in the night and were in dire need of marital navigation. Her response, a curt and clinical "You got it," did not surprise me—deflection and suppression were the lifeblood of both her existence and our marriage.

What did surprise me, at the risk of repetition, was the sheer venom and ferocity of Dana's initial assault. That attack, and the extent to which she turned her clinician's scalpel into a weapon against me, shattered any residual sense of comfort I took in her basic decency. Divorce is a sadly common occurrence. But being in possession of the emotional makeup that drives one to unleash a torrent of lies against your twenty-year partner in order to get a leg up in a coming battle for cash and prizes—and custody of the children you made together—is uncommon indeed. Manufacturing lies regarding the parenting fitness of a present and loving father is among the coldest acts one adult can impose on another.

And yet—perhaps because I knew I had not been a faithful husband and was burying decades of shame and self-loathing—my shock at her tactics was rooted in my implicit sense of her moral superiority. An old-fashioned thought, perhaps, but one which serves as a pervading inverse prejudice that speaks to the essence of the inequities of modern divorce in America. The broad notion of female moral exceptionalism—the same sentiment I harbored toward Dana— feels so deeply woven into our modern Western cultural landscape, it's as if it was embedded four levels down in our collective psyche by Leonardo DiCaprio, *Inception*-style. I see this as dangerous, because I am proof that it is not only quite easy for women to do bad things to men, but also quite common. Not only in self-defense or retaliation. Just because, like men, women are often average, run-of-the-mill human beings struggling to be good in the grey area. And they, like the rest of us, can sometimes behave horrendously and do things that would make a fictional comic book villain blush.

The Google search of "toxic masculinity" produces 8.1 million results. Google the term "toxic femininity," in contrast, and you get 1.6 million results. Included in the first page of hits are the two headlines: "There is No Such Thing as Toxic Femininity" (*Patheos*), and my personal favorite, "If you think toxic femininity is real, you are part of the problem . . ."

It is ironic that, at a time when women are making great strides toward true equality, some feminists take pains to deny the reality of toxic femininity. Surely denying the totality of the female experience includes conceding that women of every stripe exist and can be toxic in proportions equal to any man. Perhaps the most ironic and maddening trend I notice is that, even as we perpetuate the myth of moral superiority, a growing body of feminist writers eagerly (and rightfully) admonishes the worst behavior of men, but then—often in the very next paragraph—advocates for the adoption of that same bad behavior by women, assuring the reader that it's okay in this context because "it's time to fight back."

The indicators of this adoption of forsworn misconduct are not difficult to locate for anyone willing to devote even a few minutes of their time. On national radio, while promoting her book *Seven Necessary Sins*, Mona Eltahawy started the conversation with a detailed story about a real-life episode when she unleashed all the rage built up over a lifetime on a complete stranger in a nightclub, beating him relentlessly for several minutes in answer to a boorish— but minor and momentary—violation.

> Eltahawy: *"And I punched and I punched and I punched . . . and every time I thought I'd stop punching him I punched him some more."*

> Host: *"Just to be clear, you're really beating him up. It is violent."*

> Eltahawy: *"Oh yeah . . . I took it out on this man . . . and he stood up and looked me in the eye and I wasn't done and I smacked him across his jaw and almost broke my finger."*

The premise of her book is complex and intriguing. But it is not reductionist to claim that it also promotes violence and anti-civility, advocating that women use weapons she imagines are in every man's quiver, and demanding women defy, disobey, and disrupt—with complete impunity, apparently. The most confounding part of this conversation was that the radio host provided little pushback to Eltahawy's story about delivering a massive, disproportionate, criminal beating on a mostly innocent stranger. Can you imagine a mainstream book, written by a man, encouraging men to physically assault anyone they think has it coming?

There are endless articles, books, and movies about women who are lifelong victims of men; women who bounce from abusive father to abusive boyfriend. These stories are heart-wrenching and tragic. I know many women from my years in the entertainment business who had been hurt profoundly by men who were supposed to love and protect them. That there are truly bad men among us is such an obvious statement it can almost go without saying.

You will also find many stories about women who have been lifelong victims of other women—everything from the evil stepmothers and queens in ancient children's nursery rhymes to Brothers Grimm stories like *Rapunzel* and the Disney reworkings like *Tangled,* to the modern classic memoirs like Carrie Fisher's *Postcards from the Edge*—that are an unsettling staple of our culture.

Stories of men who are lifelong victims of women are more difficult to unearth. Stories of boys emotionally abused in their youth who become enslaved by their psychological scars, who are driven into the arms of women with the psychological profile perfect to continue the erosion from the inside out . . . we just don't like those stories as much. Of course, there are exceptions; Lady Macbeth was no picnic. Glenn Close boiled bunnies in *Fatal Attraction.* Crime fiction novels and film noir movies are filled with anti-heroines that are the stuff of nightmares. *Gone Girl* became a cultural touchstone a decade ago, setting fire to an explosion of stories with unreliable female narrators who lie, cheat, and kill because, in reality, we all know anyone can break bad, and every now and then we remind ourselves of that in great works of fiction. Such depictions of female predation might be exceptions to the overriding cultural zeitgeist, not the rule.

From Bias Against Women to Bias Against Men

There are undoubtedly countless reasons for this dichotomy, and specifically why male victimhood remains an ephemeral and essentially dismissed phenomenon in American culture.

My own view is that it runs counter not only to our precepts of rugged and impenetrable masculinity, but also that it confronts the reality that until recently women were, in fact, overwhelmingly the victims of prevailing social prejudice and its implications.

In the 1950s, American women in bad relationships were in a very difficult position. If a woman claimed she was being abused in her marriage, many wouldn't believe her, or they would believe her but shake their heads and shuffle away. By then, laws written and ratified by men—shaped by centuries of Western jurisprudence—had stacked up against women. Vast patriarchy conspiracies aside, most of the laws were designed with the good intention of protecting women, even while they were informed by the retrograde attitudes of the time that assumed women were in some way inferior and in need of protection. Good intentions or not, given the social realities of the world at that time, legislation often ended up creating prisons for women. They had many fewer options than men and inadequate protection from abuse. It was a claustrophobic and perverse way for marriage to be.

According to surveys at the time, the institution worked nicely for many women who enjoyed their lives with the chivalric men whose life ambitions didn't much exceed protecting and providing for their families. By and large, it wasn't bad for kids either.

Then, culturally seismic-shifting technology like "the pill"— coupled with the sexual revolution and consequently expanded expectations of women—helped usher in the women's liberation movement of the '60s and '70s, and everything we thought we understood about male-female relations changed. In America, for example, no-fault divorce made its debut in California in 1969 and only a few years later became the law in all fifty states. Many other laws that made divorce safer, fairer, and easier for women and men alike followed, and divorce swept the nation like the hula hoop. In the '50s, about 11 percent of children experienced the divorce of their parents. By the '70s, it had climbed to around 50 percent, where it has since remained. Today, there are just under a million divorces processed yearly in the United States.

Surely there can be too much of a good thing. Even the casual observer can see that, since the '70s, the advancement of women's rights has, for all its many virtues, authored a virulent strain of feminism whose effects on society have been less constructive. This aggressive subset of malignant advocacy—defined more by a nihilistic urge to emasculate men rather than escalate women—harbors ambitions to transcend mere equality to a social dominance that its adherents are convinced will only be attained once the nuclear family has been dismantled as a foundational social institution. As part of this crusade, largely due to sustained feminist activism, the Western world has endured decades of a spectacularly appalling overcorrection in family law that places men in a position every bit as destructive and oppressive as the one women faced in the '50s, albeit in different ways.

Today, two statistics stacked together tell the American story clearly. Firstly, mothers formally initiate divorce proceedings 70 percent of the time (as previously noted, 90 percent of the time for college-educated women).[17] And, secondly, when all is said and done, mothers wind up with the custody of the children nearly 83 percent of the time.[18]

---

17   Stephanie Castillo, "Evolutionary Psychology's Effect On Divorce," *Medical Daily*, August 24, 2015, https://medicaldaily.com/evolutionary-psychologys-effect-divorce-married-women-carry-historical-baggage-end-349270
18   Timothy Grall, *Custodial Mothers and Fathers and Their Child Support* (Maryland: US Census Bureau, 2016). https://census.gov/content/dam/Census/library/publications/2016/demo/P60-255.pdf

Have these numbers unearthed a magical alternate reality where women are the worthier parent 82.5 percent of the time? Of course not. Rather, they reflect a corrupt, gender-biased family law construct difficult for the average man to fight within. Most respondent fathers have lost before they ever walk into a courtroom. Two parents walk in, only one parent walks out—leaving the father a visitor.

The scope of this challenge can perhaps be understood by appreciating that even wealthy and powerful men are subject to the punitive vicissitudes of the family law typhoon. Johnny Depp, with whom I appeared in *The Pirates of the Caribbean* films, was himself tagged as the Respondent in 2016 in his split from ex-wife Amber Heard, quickly becoming TMZ fodder. Because of Depp's fame, Heard went full Reputation Savage on her way out the door, bringing the battle to the media and claiming he was a serial abuser. It then came to light that the true dynamic of their short, doomed marriage might have been something much different.

Depp, like me, is no choir boy. But, given what I've been through, I'm sure you will understand that I have no difficulty believing that—while potentially guilty of transgressions—he might also have been the victim of a campaign of defamation. He, like the rest of us, is a human being, flawed and complicated, and he deserves to be judged on the full scope of his humanity, not merely a tabloid caricature. A quick Google search of their case can provide an astounding snapshot of the destructive artfulness of someone like Heard.

I mention the Johnny Depp case because it is a powerful encapsulation of the fight in which many fathers find themselves. But his not-so-veiled warnings to Heard and her team also imply a capacity to fight for truth and reputation reparations that is not available to most fathers. The average man in America hauling home a respectable wage lives with very little or no savings and assets, so that when he is dragged to court, he simply lacks the necessary resources to climb into the ring, let alone make it through a dozen wildly prejudiced rounds in the three-ringed circus of family law.

Demonizing Masculinity is not the Solution—it's the Problem

Systemic disparity has effected a viral grip on the system, and yet there is a complete lack of internal incentives that might facilitate a return to something adjudicating American divorce with a modicum of equity and fair play. To the contrary, Dean Tong, a forensic trial consultant with decades of experience and author of multiple books about criminal allegations in US court, describes the twisted state of the existing incentive structure: "Problems of bias in family court are ubiquitous throughout Western countries and solutions are still light years away because a whole industry has built up around it with money and jobs at stake." Tong then summarizes the hurdles facing real reform: "For the mainstream media, this is a hot potato issue because the radical change needed would start a revolution."

When the System Fails with Finality

That revolution did not start with me, of course. I was just another sheep herded to the abattoir—although I had help as I was served up as the proverbial sacrificial lamb of family law. Vicki Greene's performance at my disastrous domestic violence trial, for example, was as ineffective as it was histrionic, and not entertaining enough for $850 an hour. If not for the financial assistance of a few loyal friends, I would have been bankrupt.

Once the spectacle of my trial concluded, and the inevitable verdict was issued, I quickly realized I needed new, cheaper representation. A friend had recommended the "family friendly" services of a divorce attorney named Rebecca Lizarraga.

By then I had submitted to weekly random drug tests for four months—I was essentially on perpetual call, receiving phone calls notifying me a day before. The prejudicial effect of this heavy-handed regime eviscerated what was left of my acting career. I couldn't even begin to recount how many times I had to cancel the few jobs I still managed to book because they conflicted with a test. The voice actor who cancels last minute does not get called back, and the on-camera actor who cannot guarantee his availability is never hired.

My career firmly in tatters, I glimpsed a sliver of light at the end of the tunnel as my testing requirement approached its final week. Then, the miraculous caprice of the system had its way with me yet again. I got a call one morning that final week, and promptly drove to get my test administered. On the way, I stopped at the Coffee Bean for a mocha and a lemon poppyseed muffin. I arrived soon thereafter at the facility in Sunland, a bleak bunker ten minutes off the 170 Freeway populated with sad-eyed humanity. I paid my $50 and was accompanied to the toilet by Domingo—the chap who watched me micturate to make sure I wasn't wearing a fake penis filled with synthetic body fluids—where I urinated into a plastic cup.

The following day I received a phone call.

"We have a problem with your sample," said Domingo. "You tested positive for opiates."

"There must be a mistake," I responded, dread filling my nervous system even though I wasn't sure what an opiate was.

Rebecca called me soon after. "Bogen has stopped visitation with immediate effect. Don't worry, we're going in *ex parte*."

An *ex parte* hearing, uncoupled from the legal jargon, is an emergency hearing before a judge for a quick answer about a big problem, in contrast to a regular request for orders (RFO) hearing that takes months.

"There's got to be a mistake with the testing. I didn't take a thing," I told her.

"Did you eat anything before your drug test?" asked Rebecca.

I had to think it through and came up with my snack at the coffee shop. "A coffee and a muffin," I said.

"What kind of muffin?"

"Um, lemon poppyseed."

"That could be it," she said.

Unbeknownst to me at the time, poppyseeds contain trace amounts of opiates. Armed with this information, we scrambled. I rushed to get a declaration from the server at the Coffee Bean who sold me the muffin, a credit card statement from American Express showing the purchase date and time, a toxicology report from a world-renowned Swedish toxicologist, and the results from the back-up urine sample that showed levels of opiates far below the minimum required to suggest drug use.

The next day I was in court. To make matters worse, there was a new judge assigned to the case, Bruce Iwasaki. Judge Iwasaki quickly proved himself Bogen's twisted judicial muse, ready at a moment's notice to accept her latest bombastic hyperbole and condemn me to the brig without the bother of evidence or objective hearings—not, as it turned out, a good judicial draw for me.

Bogen went in for the kill. To paraphrase her statement:

> *The respondent was found guilty of domestic violence by Judge Kaufman and ordered to submit to random drug tests once per week. His latest drug test was positive for opioids. This man. This disgrace of a man was high on opiates while driving his children and the court-appointed supervised monitor during a visit, placed them all in grave danger. Your honor, we ask that he be banned from driving the children, that he submit to twice-weekly random drug tests, and he not be afforded joint legal custody.*

All that from a poppyseed muffin. And this was *pro forma* for Bogen—some iteration of this tirade against me was fundamental to every appearance we made in court. And Iwasaki, apparently uninterested in the niceties of what actually happened, threw the book at me. My already sullied reputation was battered further as Judge Iwasaki ripped up my "golden ticket" in open court. Compounding this desultory setback, my new judicial inquisitor yanked the golden ticket Judge Kaufman extended me at the DVRO trial, making exceedingly clear that her hint at clemency and mercy was vitiated and that I should expect unreserved contempt from the court in the weeks and months to come.

That court hearing was the first in a long series in front of Judge Iwasaki that lasted three excruciating years.

The change in counsel altered the dynamic in the courtroom—no more snark and venom between the lawyers—but not the result.

Not long after I parted ways with Rebecca, she became embroiled in another case as shocking and heartbreaking as anything in fiction. In the spring of 2017, she was working for a client divorcing his wife. The ex-couple was fighting over their only son, who was five. A week after Rebecca had worked to broker a new joint-parenting schedule, her client took his son to Disneyland, then drove to a park in Santa Barbara County and smothered him to death. He sat with his son in his lap in his car for eight hours, then buried him. He then doused himself in gasoline and took pills, but passed out before he could kill himself. Later that summer, her client was sentenced to twenty-five years to life for the murder. A year later, on the anniversary of his sentencing, Rebecca drove to the place her client had killed his son and became reckless with a gun in a quiet cove. She shot into the air several times, threatening to kill herself. Police were able to de-escalate the situation without anyone getting hurt by less-than-lethal-impact weapons. The boy's mother is now suing Los Angeles County, alleging the DCFS is partly to blame for her child's death, while Rebecca is back working as a family lawyer.

Unfathomable stories like this one are, first and foremost, a tragedy for the families involved. But they hit everyone hard, especially parents who have been through the pain of a family dissolution.

An innocent child lost at the hands of a parent is unforgivable. It is the sort of crime where retributive justice is warranted. When we learn of a story like this, we think: *God, why couldn't he have just killed himself and left everyone else alone?* There's no hiding the fact that men perpetrate this kind of bone-chilling violence more than women do (eight out of ten murderers who killed a family member are men,[19] but women kill their own children at almost the same rate as men).[20]

These tragic outcomes are rare—the rate of criminal family violence of any kind (from simple assault to murder) has been cut in half in the last two decades and now involves less than two victims per 1,000.[21] But this sort of shocking tragedy is part of the reason the system is predicated on bias—because of unspeakable violence like this, when it comes to the average divorce case built on nothing more than hearsay and conjecture, common sense and evidence routinely fall by the wayside and a gross overabundance of caution is employed, causing everyone in the system to act from a place of fear and worry about being the one at the controls when a truly malevolent person slips through the cracks.

Perhaps after the shock and grief wanes, if we are going to get to a better place for our children, we need to imagine what level of pain might drive a parent—who, up until the point of doing the unthinkable exhibited no signs of malevolence—to such an extreme act of violence. As dark as the truth is, it's likely the place to reiterate the horrendous statistic from earlier in the book: men caught in the legal labyrinth of the divorce system kill themselves at epidemic proportions—a staggering eight times more often than women. Why?

At a time when so much of male behavior is pathologized by our society, many men find themselves in a Catch-22 prison that family law magnifies. On the one hand, showing natural emotional reactions to extraordinary circumstances can destroy a father's chances at getting any justice, not to mention the fact that his honesty is often met with

19   Matthew R. Durose et al, *Family Violence Statistics*, (Washington: US Department of Justice, 2005). https://bjs.gov/content/pub/pdf/fvs03.pdf

20   Dominique Bourget, MD, Jennifer Grace, MA, and Laurie Whitehurst, PhD, "A Review of Maternal and Paternal Filicide," *The Journal of the American Academy of Psychiatry and the Law* 35, no. 1 (2007): 74—82. http://jaapl.org/content/jaapl/35/1/74.full.pdf

21   Patricia Tjaden and Nancy Thoennes, Extent, *Nature, and Consequence of Intimate Partner Violence*, (Washington: Department of Justice, July 2000). https://ncjrs.gov/pdffiles1/nij/181867.pdf

lies. But on the other hand, if he contains himself within the quiet of his natural stoicism in the face of a woman emoting loudly about her victimhood, he's thrown into a war pit reserved for the Respondent, out of which he may never emerge. Women say they want a man in touch with his feelings, for example, but study after study shows that women don't like male companions who cry or display weakness. And so it is in family law: be emotional—but if you're too emotional, you will be castigated and pigeonholed, not just by other civilian men, as the myth holds, but also by women and everyone in the system.

Scanning the residual debris of my life after my experience in the system, I often find myself thinking of that five-year-old boy, lost to divorce, killed by a desperate parent, his precious life snuffed out on a node of the system just two degrees of separation away from the one I inhabit. I never met him, but I feel like I might know him better than most. He makes me think of my own boys. At the beginning of my split, my youngest boy, Smith, was eight years old. In many ways, I lost most of Smith when he was not much older than the boy that poor mother lost forever.

The patterns are undeniable. I lost my father at twelve. Dana lost her father at an even younger age. I haven't seen Smith in more than a year. As I write this book, he is fourteen. When a child of divorce asks his father why he can't be around more and is told, "If I could be there, I would be there," it makes no sense to them. Their underdeveloped brains can't conjure the densely packed matrices of madness adults can become so adept at constructing, and they think, "Well, if you wanted to be there, you would be there."

For years now I have wanted to be there for Charlie and Smith and have struggled to do everything in my power to do so, but for just as many years Dana has done everything in her power to ensure that I could not. She may not have murdered me, but she did kill me in the eyes of my sons.

To the Breaking Point and Back

The weight this steady stream of losses placed on me was beyond description, and each appearance in court heaped more salt on the already gaping wound of my irreparable separation from Charlie and Smith. Reconstructing the full chronology of hearings and applications that sealed my doom is a virtual impossibility and would take three more books to recount. Telling my story in a digestible manner entails rhetorical discipline that threatens to obscure the emotional strain of the nightmarish, *Groundhog Day*-like ride on the inescapable divorce carousel.

The tragedy that unfolded for Rebecca Lizarraga is as dark as family law offers. Even so, I had parted ways with Rebecca for my own good before that terrible episode. I understood then that, from the outside, I was beginning to look like a lawyer-jumper, but I had no choice. A paralegal who worked with Vicki and knew her berating style of lawyering firsthand recommended someone—she assured me she was friends with Judy Bogen and would be able to resolve the outstanding issues. "She never deserts clients when they run out of money," she told me. This led me to sign on with Susan Weisner.

Susan promised big plans for me and my case, starting with the services of "the best forensic accountancy firm in Los Angeles" so that we could petition the court to have Dana pay some of my attorney's fees and costs. Those big plans, of course, came at excessive cost—Susan billed me over $144,000, and the forensic accountants billed another $56,000. I was prepared to accept the economic impoverishment Susan's representation seemed to beckon, if only the results in court would shift in my direction. They didn't, of course. $200,000 bought me nothing—we lost the petition.

Undeterred, Susan shuttled me through a steady stream of additionally futile—and expensive—exercises. In response to Judge Iwasaki's twice-weekly drug test order, Susan instructed me to attend The Hills Treatment Facility and take my random drug tests there— she recommended I do four tests per week to show willingness—in lieu of the court-appointed testing facility. For months I attended daily group therapy sessions, fellowship meetings, and counseling sessions, on top of individual therapy sessions with Dr. Wood.

Susan also told me to take a hair follicle drug test to refute the opiate charge. The chemical signatures of drug use show up in hair follicles for months. Twice my drug tests came back negative, as expected.

None of it mattered—Judge Iwasaki again threw the book at me when he found out I had done as my attorney instructed and attended The Hills. Far from seeing it as the proactive step Susan had promised, he vilified me for "thinking I knew better than the court" and "ignoring his orders." I sat, helpless and hopeless, as the judge castigated me. The fact that Dana was served with over 100 counts of contempt of various orders was an immateriality to Iwasaki, whose Bogen-inspired inquisition continued.

What Mad Hatter's Tea Party did I find myself in? I had followed the instructions of my attorney, but it only further damaged my character in the eyes of the court. It was one of the most insane things about being stuck in a high-priced legal battle: even following the advice of a thousand-dollar-an-hour expert might produce horrible results.

Susan next put me in touch with an attorney named Beatrice Fung who specialized in cases involving the DCFS. Since I had been found guilty of child abuse based on the initial hearsay allegation that had been used as the basis to convict me of domestic violence, Beatrice informed me that I had been placed on the Child Abuse Central Index (CACI) as well that of the Department of Justice (DOJ).

The timing of my initial contact with Beatrice was notable, considering it had been six months since I had been found guilty of domestic violence. Those six months had been the worst of my life—they were a blur of hearings, and now I faced the specter of a hearing to renew the restraining order, a marker that I suspected would force me to relive the whole hellacious experience.

In the whirlwind leading up to the court hearings, I did get some good news from Beatrice. In a stunning reversal, she informed me that the DCFS had canceled my grievance hearing and, after an internal review, decided to modify their original report. My name would be expunged from the criminal databases. Thank God—or whatever higher being might be listening—for small miracles.

I happily took the brief respite from the stream of bad news and setbacks, but the damage to my reputation, career, and relationship with my boys was already done. And the respite was particularly short lived, because among the materials delivered with the expungement order was the initial fifty-six-page report to which I'd been denied access before Judy Bogen strolled into court and set her sights on me. This was the report the DCFS deliberately dispatched to my former home—knowing I would not see it and thus would be unable to respond within the fourteen-day deadline—and which, until now, I'd yet to lay eyes on. Reading it was to relive the tumult of those harrowing days in March 2015. It excruciatingly detailed the "investigation" that had been conducted, and the horrendous questions DCFS personnel had asked Charlie and Smith—"Did Daddy ever touch your penis?" being among the candidates for most repulsive. But for all its toxic tenor, this report, authored by the same DCFS agent that had spared no effort to keep me incarcerated, exonerated me of any child abuse or wrongdoing on March 5, 2015! This exculpatory report, finally delivered and received, acknowledged my innocence under the law but was powerless to save me from the assassination of my character the system had already effectuated. No wonder the grievance hearing had been cancelled on short notice. There was no "internal review." No report "modification" had taken place. This DCFS agent had documented my innocence in the original report, at the end of March 2015, yet knowingly withheld it from me and my legal representatives.

What did this all mean? It meant I was not a child abuser. Nor was I a drug addict. And the DCFS knew that from the outset. You will forgive me if, in reading this long suppressed report, I confess to a sense of vindication. The truth was slowly forcing its way through the cracks in the hard, cold floor that Judy, Dana and her mother, and the system in general, had installed on my life.

But I soldiered on and, in March of 2016, walked once more into Department 63 at the Stanley Mosk Courthouse in downtown LA, desperate to clear my name, this time prepared to contest Dana's request for renewal of the restraining order and armed and ready to present the "not guilty" DCFS findings for the first time. Things did not go as planned.

Bogen began the proceedings by presenting an unopened American Express bill and insinuated that I had mailed it to Dana as a financial threat (I had not). Susan mentioned that two weeks previously, Bogen had sent a disturbing letter explaining that she had filed a report with the Beverly Hills Police Department accusing me of breaking in, burglarizing, and ransacking her home. The charge was preposterous, and quite laughable—one made by an infamous LA divorce lawyer with enough enemies to leave Al Capone blushing, trying to pin a robbery on me with zero evidence. But such is Judy's relentless game. That particular Bogen shenanigan cost me over $10,000 in legal fees.

Yet another disaster. Susan didn't even bring up the DCFS findings that exonerated me! Her response was, effectively, to wave the white flag and concede. She said as much, all but inviting Judge Iwasaki to extend the existing restraining order. There I was, watching my lawyer give up in open court. Judge Iwasaki granted Dana's request for a renewal based on my alleged mail intimidation—another year of ordered restraint, of being prohibited from going anywhere near my home, contacting Dana, communicating with my sons, visiting their school, or taking part in their lives in any way.

Susan, fresh off her surrender, then dropped another bomb on me. She announced she was resigning from my case, moments before taking a seat in her shiny, black, chauffeur-driven Bentley that whisked her away. I was left once again lacking legal representation to defend me from the madness, only this time $300,000 in the hole to compound financial insult to my legal injury.

The problem was that it was too late to help me, and nobody cared. The truth was that I was the victim of an elaborate, efficient perfidy machine that had succeeded in beating me down and placing me on the perpetual defensive. Each time I cleared myself of one false charge, the next was waiting in the wings. In family law, such significant moments of injustice are nothing more than a clerical keystroke to those who live in this world.

I wasn't a child abuser or a drug addict, but defending myself in family court had now become a full-time career. My life was consumed by therapy, drug testing, legal paperwork, court deadlines, the pressures of monitored visitation, and a mind-numbing legal hourly rate. Judy was relentless—practically every day she peppered me with letters full of bombastic, exaggerated rhetoric that paved new pathways to the courthouse, each one requiring an official letter in response from my attorney to set the story straight. I could no longer cope with it all. I was stretched to my limit and barely holding on. The wild west of family law takes no prisoners.

Judge me as you may, but I have more than once found myself watching the sentencing hearing for Rebecca's client who smothered his son on YouTube. The boy's mother was in agony as she told her ex-husband in her address to the court how she felt about the fact that she would never see her boy again.

"I hope you relive the image of murdering my baby every day of your insignificant life," she told him. "May your dark soul burn in eternal hell."

I watched her despairing and cried for her. I can relate to the pain, though it may be difficult for some to understand. It is hard to accept that losing a child to divorce involves a level of pain akin to losing a child to death, and granted, spending too much more time making comparisons is macabre and unproductive. I suspect many psychologists will agree that knowing your children are alive and well although unable to be with you—especially when the reasons for the prohibition have largely been disproven or dismissed—involves a depth of profound bereavement that, irrespective of whether it approximates death, is agonizing in ways that cannot be explained or understood unless through experience.

• • •

That pain, and the cumulative emotional toll of the process, reached its zenith for me on the afternoon of May 11, 2016. The grief of losing the daily connection with my sons was too much for me to bear. I walked out of my modest Hollywood rental in the general direction of the palatial estate that had been the culmination of a lifetime of my work. I wanted to be with my sons and nothing else mattered. I walked into traffic, oblivious of the cars screeching out of the way. A sense of impenetrability overwhelmed me. For a man who has always obsessed about the details, the particulars of this situation seemed distant—I had reached a point where life and death fused, where I surrendered my fate to the universe, knowing it was indifferent to my plight. I marched across Cahuenga Boulevard. I saw the oncoming traffic but couldn't feel it. I headed directly towards the bridge over the 101 at Barham Boulevard, and certain death.

I would see my sons again, and nothing would stop me. I would exorcise my demons and redeem my soul. I was God-like in my vulnerable strength. Death was barely an abstraction—it might frustrate my immediate journey in this life but could not, in my mind, derail the mission before me and reclaim what had been stolen from me, the only thing with meaning to me—my sons. The concrete barrier separating Cahuenga Boulevard from the long drop to Highway 101 below was now the only thing impairing my momentum. I stared at the trees of Lakeside Golf Club in the distance—beyond which lay my family residence—overcome with the inescapability of the unbearable trauma and unrelenting living grief of being separated from the meaning of my life—my beautiful boys.

While I was focused on the reclamation of my soul, a cashier at a convenience store across the street had seen me embark on my would-be homecoming and became concerned. He burst across Cahuenga to stop me dead in my tracks. This humble man—Jason Leif—who didn't know me and had no stake in my life, had nevertheless made it his business to save me.

And in that moment, death was snuffed out by a stranger—a man working beyond logic, following ancient instinctual imperatives to save a lost soul.

Fate is indeed fickle, but mine, as it transpired, had not yet been sealed.

GENTLE MIND

Arrest the mind, detain the thinking,
Save the wounded child from sinking.
Unpack the cruel, release the kind,
Be still in body, gentle mind.

Hate the timid in-timid haters,
Self-intervention of cyclic natures.
Grading the no-man's land of my psychic paradigm,
Aligning, refining, re-defining the mind-monster,
Protecting my introspection.

Rejection of journeying to another trauma pocket dimension,
With positive purpose and intention.
Revealing tenacity,
A deep capacity,
To unpack the cruel,
Release the kind,
Be still in body, gentle mind.

CHAPTER 11

THE MASS KIDNAPPING OF AMERICAN CHILDREN

"We have two lives. The second begins the moment we realize we have only one."

How was it that I reached a point of such despair that I found myself on an overpass, glaring at the traffic below, indifferent to my own physical plight and prepared to dive headfirst into that mass of moving metal? I would have struggled to cobble together a lucid response then, aside from the obvious effect of fourteen months' losses in divorce court. Detailing the monotonous repetition of events that prevailed in court, the death of my fatherhood, and the slow undoing of my will to continue, is beyond my capacity to reduce to a single book. But in May of 2016, all I could do was *feel* the suffering the system had inflicted on me. My subsequent journey, for its false starts and turbulence, occasioned an *understanding* of how Dana authored my demise in ways I simply could not appreciate as it was happening. That understanding shakes me to the core to this day and makes me gravely concerned for the next poor scapegoat, fleeced and dragged through the meat grinder.

. . .

"Dad, remember when you used to sing songs and tell us stories at bedtime and you always said, 'Good night my boys. Sweet dreams. Mummy and daddy love you very much?'"

"Yes. Such lovely memories, aren't they?"

"Mum doesn't do that. She hugs me and Charlie and keeps saying to us over and over, 'Tell me that you love me. I need to hear that you love me.' She squeezes us so tight we can't breathe and won't let us go to sleep until we've said, 'I love you, mom' over and over again."

Charlie then chimed in, adding to the depressing portrait Smith was painting of life inside my erstwhile home. "I smile to keep Mum happy", he offered, "because she asks me every day if I love her . . . But I'm crying inside," he confided. "The house feels empty without you," he continued, as the sharp pain in my chest intensified. "Mum is haunting the house," he concluded, and "I hate her for it."

Devastating. And illuminating in its punishing simplicity. This conversation with the boys punctuated one of my first visits with them in 2015. It was among the first clear warnings that, even if I managed the impossible and moved through the minefield of divorce without a misstep, it was still going to be a horrendous journey for my children.

During my most recent chaperoned visit with my kids in late 2019—one of only a handful in the past five years—my kids, after having been denied their cell phones throughout years of visits, both showed up holding their phones in front of their faces. I was informed later that one of them may have been wearing a hidden body cam. Had Dana conscripted our son, in the midst of our dispute, as an unwitting mule to capture and transmit damaging information about me, his father? The depths of Dana's contempt, and the extent to which her parental priorities had become distorted, were laid bare in this episode. My destruction and humiliation were all that mattered to her—all else existed only in service of that purpose.

Parental Alienation is Child Abuse

I came to realize what I was ignorant of at the start of this process: my sons and I were the victims of extreme parental alienation. Over several years, they were relentlessly, systematically manipulated into believing that I was a broken and dangerous man who should be hated and not trusted. This was all notwithstanding that I had been examined extensively by multiple psychiatrists and psychologists, all of whom gave me a completely clean bill of health (clear-eyed psychological assessments that do not come easily or cheaply; they took hours, cost tens of thousands of dollars and, more distressing, proved no utility whatsoever to my cause). In the process, Charlie and Smith were denied the basic human right to have me as a father, and I was denied my right to be a father to them. I am now an erased parent.

In 2019, the World Health Organization (WHO) officially recognized parental alienation as a mental health issue damaging to children. Parental alienation is a profoundly complex psychological affliction that has been allowed to flourish through a complicated interplay between our modern—and often wrong—views on society, men and women, family, and child psychology.

The WHO, along with countless other medical and psychological practitioners and the associations that promote and govern them, are finally saying what many have known for decades: parental alienation is child abuse. Because family court is ground zero for family dissolution, and family dissolution provides a parent the necessary physical breach to engage in brainwashing, it is easy to understand that a broken legal system decades behind in psychological and social science actually encourages this form of psychological abuse. It is even more telling that the WHO's main opponents to seeking official recognition of parental alienation as a psychological scourge were feminist groups.

Parental alienation is a part of divorce steeped in maddeningly nebulous psychological jargon rendering the underlying information impenetrable. For instance, the WHO describes parental alienation as "substantial and sustained dissatisfaction within a caregiver-child relationship associated with significant disturbance in functioning."

I learned that parental alienation is sometimes referred to as "malicious mother syndrome" because women are more often found to engage in its behaviors. The diagnostic criteria for divorce-related malicious mother syndrome reads as a veritable blueprint for Dana's successful assault on me:

1. A mother who unjustifiably punishes her divorcing or divorced husband by:
   - attempting to alienate their mutual child(ren) from the father;
   - involving others in malicious actions against the father;
   - engaging in excessive litigation.[22]

2. A mother who specifically attempts to deny her child(ren):
   - regular, uninterrupted visitation with the father;
   - uninhibited telephone access to the father;
   - paternal participation in the child(ren)'s school life and extracurricular activities.

3. The mother's behavior is pervasive and includes malicious acts towards the husband, such as:
   - telling the child(ren) lies about the father;
   - telling others lies about the father;
   - acting against the father in ways that violate the law.

4. The syndrome is not specifically due to another mental disorder, but another disorder may coexist (in Dana's case, panic disorder).

---

22   Ira Daniel Turkat, Ph.D., "Divorce-Related Malicious Mother Syndrome," *The Journal of Family Violence*, 10, No. 3 (1995): 253-264. http://fact.on.ca/Info/pas/turkat01.htm#:~:text=The%20proposed%20definition%20encompasses%20four,malicious%20actions%20against%20the%20father

Chills assemble at the base of my spine when I read this clinical, nearly academic description of precisely what happened to me. Translated into plain English, parental alienation is where a spiteful and/or mentally ill parent brainwashes a child to reject and hate the other parent.

Dana conscripted our boys into every single one of these targeted attacks on me, and there was nothing I could do because the professionals of the family law system were either inadequately trained to spot the signs, or would simply turn a blind eye to them.

I endured systematic alienation from Smith and Charlie as Dana hijacked my relationship with them. Week after agonizing week, I was a forced participant in the process of being dissociated from my boys. They would arrive for a visit, chaperoned by the desultory monitor, and for the ensuing two hours it would become clear that Dana had enlisted all three as agents in her war against me. The boys would ask strange, pointed questions, clearly at Dana's instruction and with the understanding that the answers would be reported back to her— with the monitor serving as a would-be court reporter, recording every word.

"I just want to live a normal life. A mom and dad, in a home," Smith had told me. This comment was made during the same visit where Smith had informed me that, "Mum got a trained Germen shepherd attack dog. She said it's to kill you if you come to the house." Upon arrival for the following week's visit I was shocked to see bruises, scars and stitches on Smith's face. The dog had apparently pinned Smith down and mauled him, causing unspeakable psychological trauma. (At the hospital he had to be held down by restraints because he was so hysterical. Dana chose not to inform me.)

"We're scared for Mosely," said Smith. Mosely was our family dog, a boxer puppy I'd brought home when the boys were six and four years old. The new dog didn't like her.

Dana had been ordered by the judge to allow Mosely to join the boys on our visits, but after only a few occasions she put an end to that. Four years later, at the bottom of an email from her attorney, was a p.s. Mosely died. This news, and the method of delivery, was another emotional blow that was hard to recover from. Having been denied access to my boys, as well as my dog, I was now forced to imagine how Mosely had died, how much pain she may have been in, and where she was finally laid to rest.

The dance was dizzying because all I wanted was to connect with the boys. Dana may have been the one that made the trains run on time, but I had always been the boys' emotional anchor. Judge Kaufman, and even Judge Iwasaki—who seemed to receive my every utterance as confirmation of a deeply held contempt for me—acknowledged the close emotional bond I shared with the boys. But I walked into family court the first day of my DVRO trial a parent and walked out a soon-to-be stranger, an estrangement which grew more and more acute as the weeks and the visits mounted. It wasn't merely the questions aimed to set me up for a later kill in court—where Bogen could recite, or mis-cite, my response as evidence of my parental unfitness—but also the look of fear in the boys' eyes. Dana had convinced them I was dangerous and that I alone was responsible for all the instability they had experienced since March 5.

There were no options at my disposal to arrest the descent. The system had tagged me a threat to the boys the night of March 5, and now its machinery consolidated that designation, regardless of my protests of innocence. Melissa Isaak, a veteran family lawyer in the state of Alabama and head of a firm specializing in defending men in contested divorce, described my exact feelings when she observed, "It's almost as if the Constitution is suspended in family court. People don't understand that in the family law arena, domestic violence is used as a tool. Essentially, the silver bullet is the best way to destroy your opponent and win the game . . . and women use this far more than men, in my experience."

I had unwittingly succumbed to that Silver Bullet, and I didn't realize at first that I'd been hit, or the terminal injuries I had suffered. Divorce court chooses its victims deliberately and administers its venom with a stealthy reserve.

CHAPTER 12

A CRUSADE OF
FAMILIAL GENOCIDE

"Victory is meaningless if you're fighting the wrong battle."

Sil·ver Bul·lets: simple, *seemingly* magical solutions to difficult problems.

Anyone who balks at analogies between war and a toxic divorce with a bad faith petitioner has simply not experienced it themselves. The Silver Bullet paradigm is a war-fighting philosophy, aimed at crippling the opponent before the conflict really begins. And while it is a war waging in miniature to anyone looking in from the outside, it's an all-encompassing global conflict to those forced to fight for hearth and home; the stakes involve nothing less than your future, your freedom, your children, your home, and maybe even your life.

It also rewards—as I have recounted based on my own experience—the bold and those willing to strike first and with stealth. On December 6, 1941, Japanese diplomats engaged in peace talks with their American counterparts in Washington D.C. At the moment those talks broke, the Japanese Armada had been at sea for ten days and was preparing to launch an attack the next morning that would spark America's involvement in World War II, and incite the dawning of the American century—Pearl Harbor. The American diplomats believed they were negotiating peace. The Japanese diplomats, however, were engaged in a strategic ruse, inducing their American counterparts to invest in the peace process at the very moment they were preparing to launch a war.

The scope of this diplomatic deception was profound, but to extend the metaphor to its logical conclusion, this is precisely the form of deception that Dana inflicted on me, and which is the foundation of the family law system. Deceive and subdue your spouse (soon to be the enemy) to complacency during the prelude to hostilities while setting in motion an attack at the same time.

The Six Silver Bullets of High Conflict Divorce

No one I know who has endured this process has not come out the other side deeply traumatized. The Silver Bullet in this maze of madness is the false allegation that I have spoken so much about.

My journey into the dystopian nightmare of high conflict divorce actually included six Silver Bullets speeding at me in quick succession, like that infamous scene in *The Matrix*—except with me displaying reaction times akin to those of the dead guy in *Weekend at Bernie's,* as opposed to the magic bullet-dodging game of Neo.

These collective munitions of high-conflict divorce have become the battle-tested superweapons for disgruntled spouses who want to get rid of their primary partners immediately, and men in particular are vulnerable to their force. They debilitate husbands and can prove deadly to fathers. Such is their lethality that I have read of many men who, facing the crosshairs, have taken their own lives as a result.

Fathers, husbands, and men in crisis who have or may unwittingly become the Respondent are branded the familial black sheep, the proverbial systemic scapegoat, targeted by a Reputation Savage and shot through with these Silver Bullets.

Scape·goat: a person blamed for the faults of others, especially for reasons of expediency.

At their conceptual core, the six Silver Bullets are projectiles forged with innate, deeply ingrained psychological compounds; primed with the incendiary intergenerational dogma of the shooter's family system of origin; encased in the human kryptonite of anticipatory shame and propelled by reputation savagery—word of mouth, hearsay, made-up stories, and spoken truth inversions.

In the hands of one devoted to destruction and retribution, the chamber unloads like this:

Silver Bullet 1: The Incarcerating Incident

This is the false allegation at the core of my story. A menace to every Respondent, the incarcerating incident is the moment when the stealth attack is revealed in the sunlight. The unsuspecting perpetrator, bathed in smug ignorance, becomes the victim, tagged with a defining mark that will haunt him for the remainder of the proceeding. No amount of context, explanation, or exculpatory evidence can overcome the emotional impact of the incarcerating incidence. Once a perp, always a perp. And the "perp" rarely expects the opprobrium that comes with his newfound title—he is blind to the coming tsunami of both legal and figurative contempt and thus cannot reconcile himself to the inverted circumstances in which he finds himself. By the time he regains his footing, he is swept under a ferocious current and the only imperative is bare, raw survival. All else must give way.

Mine was a particularly apropos example of this principle. Dana's swiftness and efficiency in having me detained and designated a threat to the boys placed me in a legal canyon that I could never traverse. My ability to contest the divorce—or meaningfully fight for my rights as a father—were effectively exterminated before I ever walked into a courtroom.

Silver Bullet 2: The Order of Restraint

This is the legal equivalent of a film treatment, the moment when the basic morality play of every divorce is scripted in short form. The Respondent is a danger, threatening to his spouse, and thus is eternally condemned. Then comes the second sucker punch. The whole dynamic shifts once the scarlet letter of a protection order is seared on your chest. There is now a paper trail indicating that you are dangerous or unworthy. You have been made the villain, and it's now incumbent upon you to prove otherwise. Temporary restraining orders abound, obtained quickly and easily—but only 15 percent of temporary orders are replaced with permanent orders after further examination by the courts, and that might tell you all you need to know about the validity of the temporary ones. Protection orders rip you from your home, your worldly possessions, your routine, your friends and neighbors, and your children. The firing of Silver Bullet 2 increases the potency and lethality of Bullets 3, 4, and 5 exponentially.

Again, Dana proved a skillful practitioner of this component of the faux melodrama of divorce court. She quickly seized on my detention and nefarious designation—both based on falsehoods she perpetrated—and slapped a restraining order on me before my mind had cleared the cobwebs of the Del Amo nightmare, swiftly hammering another permanent nail into my coffin.

Silver Bullet 3: The Security Lock

After securing the family home, the securing of everything else must immediately follow. Change all the locks, passwords, and codes. Put a virtual lockbox around the world, cutting the cord to children, devices, and paperwork. No computer, no cell phone, no connection.

Chalk up another notch on Dana's championship belt—she accomplished each of these with withering speed.

Silver Bullet 4: The Private Investigation

Now amateurs and professionals alike can commence the poking and prodding detective work. Knowledge is power and information is paramount. The Petitioner dispatches the CIA of family war, the "Untouchable Cartel" of private Investigators—third-party facilitators who seek to promote and propagate the conflict.

In my case, when it wasn't Dana or her mother, professionals were deployed to do their dirty work. Private eyes float around the fringes of the courts, experts at exploiting the cracks in the system and more than willing to commit crimes for lawyers who don't want dirt on their hands. Dana went for the jugular here, as she did at every opportunity in our case. She retained the services of a dark master of the marriage dissolution arts named John Nazarian, a private investigator who once created a series of YouTube videos with titles like, "How to Get Your Husband Arrested." He is a California barracuda adept at helping disgruntled spouses fire off Bullets 1 and 2.

But Nazarian's presence wasn't merely nefarious in my case, it was genuinely bizarre because, alas, and in a particularly toxic "coincidence," I eventually discovered he was related to the monitor whom Dana and Judy had asked the court to appoint to accompany me on my visits with Charlie and Smith.

You cannot make this stuff up. The monitor, Michael Valdavinos, was a dour young man who betrayed no apparent personality, but who routinely appeared at my doorstep—with the boys in tow—in new cars, typically tricked-out SUVs with a self-consciously meretricious look to them. I labored to forge some kind of relationship with him, but he would have none of it. Were that all of it, I would be sick to my stomach. But there's more, amazingly. Valdavinos was . . . wait for it . . . the offspring of John Nazarian, the PI who Dana had hired to turn over every stone of my life.

That extraordinary connection to Nazarian, Dana's investigatory hitman, was never disclosed to me. I uncovered it doing a spot of my own amateur sleuthing, which I was prompted to do after three years of my visits with the boys being disrupted by Nazarian's process servers handing me legal papers—in the boys' presence—on Judy Bogen and Dana's behalf. I initially was too overwhelmed to consider the fact that Nazarian always seemed, uncannily, to know my whereabouts while I was on these Valdavinos-monitored visits. But over time the frequency of these disruptions were simply too great to be a coincidence, and I became suspicious. That suspicion was compounded by Valdavinos's arrogance and contempt for any sense of protocol and fair play. He unilaterally changed the means of my payment, announcing at one point that he would no longer accept checks. He would demand payment for amounts that were not yet due, under threat of canceling pending visits. After the infamous poppyseed muffin incident and the court prohibiting me from driving the boys myself, Valdavinos suddenly informed me that he would no longer drive me and the boys on any visits, blaming this inexplicable change on his insurance company— that change, notwithstanding that he had previously imposed a car cleaning fee on me by which I paid to have his various gangster SUVs cleaned after every visit, left me entirely captive to him during the visits. And, as if to emphasize the middle finger he so enjoyed directing my way, he would cancel visits minutes before the boys' scheduled arrival and then charge me for the visits he had canceled.

All of which heightened my suspicion of what was transpiring, and facilitated my fleeting foray into the dark world of investigation. There I discovered not only Valdavinos's paternity, but a great deal more about this obviously troubled individual whom Dana and Bogen had placed in charge of the boys. He apparently had a past criminal history, maintained a long series of aliases, and used to be a woman called Sonya. I repeat, this tale is beyond the capacity of the human imagination. It seems impossible, and yet it's true. And while I'm not one to challenge the scruples of another man, if I were a wagering bloke I would lay down my life savings—an admittedly paltry sum after being almost cleaned out during my stint at Del Amo—on the proposition that Valdavinos reported everything he observed on my visits to Nazarian. An incestuously toxic stew, and Rod Serling would have rejected it as too outrageous for *The Twilight Zone*. But this was the man whom Dana wanted driving the boys around and monitoring my visits with them. Welcome to the Mad Hatter's Tea Party.

So, be keenly sensitive to Silver Bullet 4, because the private investigation might not only entail your soon-to-be-ex-wife ripping through your computer files and performing all sorts of insidious actions with your finances, but additionally placing a veritable mole in your midst in the form of a monitor with a connection to the investigator, which brings me to Silver Bullet 5.

Silver Bullet 5: The Financial Recounting

Creative bookkeeping that would make even the hardened cynic whistle is central to the pre-packaged destruction at the core of the divorce strategy. A cunning divorcée gets to this early and finishes the job after you are kicked out of your home. She and a team of forensic accountants cook the books some more, slicing and dicing the spoils of a lifetime of work. With the proper team at work, a financial picture can be bent into any shape. This creative historical bookkeeping is done in preparation to slant the diss-o-master—the computer software program used in family law proceedings that generates support guidelines based primarily on a party's earnings and time share with the children, often in favor of the Petitioner.

Dana, at the risk of repetition, made quick work of our finances, appropriating all our bank accounts and passwords while I desperately sought escape from Del Amo. I was, from that point on, at her financial mercy—and she showed me none.

Silver Bullet 6: The Legal Retention

While I put this bullet last, it often comes first—the Respondent does not feel the pain until the other five bullets land. It is a stealth team of pros that packages and presents the results of the onslaught. It is the most awe-inspiring inversion of victimhood, the ultimate offensive team pretending to play defense. By the time this team of legal gunslingers ties everything up in a twisted bow, the Respondent is bleeding out on the floor, riddled with subversive shots.

In my case, Dana hired Judy Bogen.

The new social currency is victimhood, and its economy is booming.

This weaponized blueprint is, theoretically, gender neutral on its face. But no matter what you've been led to believe, my direct experience—and my extensive research of the broader system—is that the majority of the violent destruction of a family is done by women. I can hear some say, "That's correct, sir! Smart women have learned they don't have to accept a bad situation. They are going to exercise their right to walk from the oppressive marriage institution if they're not getting what they need."

That sounds pretty lean-in-cool and girl-power-chic, but if this empowerment was at the heart of it all, then these strong, modern women would be willing to walk away from the marriage carrying only what they brought into it and agreeing to a 50/50 parenting arrangement for the good of the kids. They would not become the Petitioner, sheltering themselves in victimhood and blanket immunity. They would not explode from the line with minds full of premeditated subterfuge, preconscious betrayal, and dark visions of winning the gold medal in the Limbic Olympics of family law.

All of which is to say that women—particularly smart, educated women—may have won the battle while losing the broader war. They have harnessed the plentiful tools of the family law system to empower themselves in its peculiar vacuum and exact breathtaking retribution on their former partner's life. But in doing so, they may be perpetuating the conceit of a victimhood culture, one conserving the very social presumptions the women's movement has fought against for decades. The result is tragedy and victimhood for everyone. This name-blame-and-shame game is now pathologized in the institutional monster.

That said, the system provides little incentive for women to evolve their present strategy. Were it rooted in a genuine search for truth, and not rotting with institutional prejudice, perhaps the Petitioners would lay down the smoking gun and put their doomed relationship out of its misery humanely. But it instead facilitates a synthetic morality play, where the threat potential of men is metastasized into a virtually irrebuttable presumption of actual menace—hence, an imaginary crime immediately becomes, in the eyes of the authorities, true by mere virtue of a woman making a charge against a man. Due process is for chumps.

So it was for me, writ large. I had no history of violence, no criminal record, no prior arrests, and there were zero instances of physical abuse in our twenty years of marriage. Dana's first Silver Bullet, the incarcerating incident, was purely a figment of her imagination—a fabrication with no morsel of evidence. And yet, the consequences to me were devastatingly incalculable.

• • •

I am one of millions of men who have suffered this fate, a statistical blip in a system built on my destruction and that of others like me. The problem is not simply the mechanics of family law—it strikes deep into the core of social pathology, and how men have become this corroded patriarchal caricature. The "frenzy whip" of collective Munchausen-by-proxy is evident in our modes of relating. There is currently no event horizon of apology in our present public discourse, as echoed in the smoke-and-mirror chambers of the adversarial family law system and amplified in our cancel culture wars.

The Silver Bullets strategy exploits this convenient and dismissive generalization and is so successful because of the power of social conceits. It is the ultimate magic trick, where only the magician knows the secret to the hoodwink. Even if the magician chooses not to reveal the trick, the audience believes them. They never see where the cards really are. They know it cannot be magic, yet when the effect is presented perfectly, it works like a charm.

And, like all magic, it leaves you questioning what is real. After Dana fired the first Silver Bullet, I still believed in miracles. I still trusted Dana; I refused to believe she would betray that trust. I give her credit for that, but the speed with which she moved to destroy me has—despite its strategic and tactical merit—shattered any residual belief I had in the choices we'd made and the life we'd built. She had obliterated all of it with such a withering indifference to the consequences that I could no longer trust the propriety of anything we'd promised each other, or the boys.

That notion of trust is critical, because trust is a basic biological necessity. It is impossible to imagine functioning as living organisms if we live in mistrust of each other. We could not only *not* make a choice, but we could not act effectively. Before we can make a choice and act, some degree of surety and faith must exist.

Once shattered, however, reconstructing the psychology necessary to trust is an immense challenge. If you're a husband or father jettisoned into the noxious firestorm of high-conflict divorce, hold on tight to your faculties, dig deep into your emotional resources, and prepare to be pulverized in ways you could never conceive if your life depended on it (which it does). I have been in your positional purgatory; I have experienced the unrelenting death squads of family law, who pile up the bodies and line their pockets for their needy, greedy "greater good." The system has scant mercy for good fathers and offers little, if any, meaningful relief to any male Respondent. I have endured, and continue to endure, the trust crisis that naturally accompanies this pathological system.

Rest assured, you are not mad. You are not insane. You are just stuck in an adversarial system whose sole purpose is to *represent* you as insane. Family law is, in that regard, a reflection of our society's collective shadow self, and currently suffers from a pathogen of madness perspective.

per·spec·tivo mad·ness: an attitude or point of view that someone else is severely mentally ill.

CHAPTER 13

THE EX-COMMUNICATOR

*"Life isn't about waiting for the storm to pass.
It's about learning to dance in the rain."*

I am compelled to detail my own experience and attempt to place it in a broader context because the parental alienation dynamic is impossible to explain to anyone who has not been subjected to it. The psychological damage this behavior inflicts on our children is immeasurable. A growing body of research illuminates the effects of this form of abuse, but the basic import is this: the dynamic invites self-hatred and self-esteem issues, higher rates and risks of depression, relationship difficulties, substance abuse, loss of guidance and support, loss of relationship with extended family, and an inability to develop and sustain healthy relationships.

This form of alienation is complex, to be sure, and the symptoms can be difficult to see because the dynamics present in an extremely counterintuitive fashion. But every parent—every divorcing father in particular—is susceptible to this seemingly irreversible alienation. My research demonstrates that my suffering was hardly unique, but redressing the situation is an immense challenge, because as Harvard

Medical School faculty member and parental alienation expert Dr. Steven Miller explains, parental alienation can be difficult to spot. In a divorce steeped in an alienation dynamic, he says, most of the professionals involved in the process "will not only get the evaluation wrong, but they will get it exactly backwards." This, he says, is because the psychology at play is not all that different from the infamous "Stockholm Syndrome" from films and literature, in which the victimized person comes to identify, love, and defend their captor over time.

In parental alienation, the perpetrating parent is not only a master manipulator, but—often due to problems stemming from childhood trauma—also has a pathological, unnatural enmeshment with the child, to the point where he or she "has lost his or her individuality" and experienced an erosion of their critical reasoning skills.

According to Dr. Miller, this enmeshment—frequently invisible to the untrained observer—takes the form of infantilization, where the perpetrator treats the child like a baby and doesn't allow them to grow into age-appropriate activities and friendships. Other times, it involves the "adultification" or "spousification" of the child, including treating them like grown-ups, oversharing details of the divorce, and trashing the character of the other parent. This is what happened in my case.

The deceptive aspects of severe parental alienation can run colder and further than that, Dr. Miller says, and to understand how, one must consider the concept of a fundamental attribution error. For example, upon seeing an angry father, we are hardwired to think: "That man is angry due to a defect in his character," not "That man is angry because someone just stole his car." As I argued in the preceding few chapters, our society has become even further biased, to the point where we have been trained to perceive the identical conduct in men and women as entirely distinct in implication. Thus, an angry father is presumptively a bad person, but a mother exhibiting the same anger elicits no similar reflexive judgment. To the contrary, she is commonly assumed to be reacting to a negative stimulus—like an angry father.

This dynamic is deadly in divorce proceedings. When an alienating parent adept at manipulation walks into court, says Dr. Miller, she might present as "cool, calm, and collected." In contrast, the targeted parent might have post-traumatic stress disorder, may not have seen his kids for months or years, and might have been subjected to a powerful, durable, and enervating character assassination campaign. He might walk into a hearing feeling stressed, vulnerable, anxious, and angry, and he gets clobbered by experts who aren't trained in this form of abuse. In my case, as in so many others, my ex-wife was portrayed in court as a traumatized victim. Once through the courtroom doors, her demeanor would change from delicate, trampled flower to towering anger, marching down the courthouse corridor sneering at me.

Allow me to return to the father suicide statistic. Surely, we would be remiss if we were not to imagine that at least part of the reason fathers are eight times more likely to commit suicide during or after divorce might be because they are fighting through nothing less than a state-sanctioned kidnapping campaign—wouldn't we?

The Devaluation of Marriage and Family

In living through my described ordeals and in writing this book, I repeatedly returned to the same question: *how did we get here?* How could we, living in a country uniquely rooted in the individual rights of its citizens to resist the tyrannical urges of the state, arrive at a place where those very rights feel suspended the moment one walks into family court?

The reasons are undoubtedly complex, but if you're like me and so many others, you sense we're at a point where our attempts to discuss the issues foundational to a healthy society—including our pitiful war between the sexes—are desperate for a massive dose of humility from the Gods. We need to question how we built a system that so callously breaks down our core relationships and principles and blocks the pathways to redemption and apology.

I am dismayed at the tenor of much of the discussion about the nuclear family. Marriage appears, to my eyes, to be on life support, and yet I see many who appear happy about it. Even while a backbone narrative of this COVID-19 pandemic involves families hunkered down in quarantine, the statistics reveal the decay of marriage as a foundational institution. As I write this, *The Wall Street Journal* reports that, according to the National Center for Health Statistics, the US marriage rate has plunged to 6.5 new unions per 1,000 people, the lowest level since the government began recording these statistics in 1867. Of course, a plunging quantity of marriages says nothing of quality, and one might argue that fewer good marriages is better than a greater number of bad ones—but the trend speaks to the erosion of the belief that marriage is a social institution that leads to a better outcome for children.

Celebrated *New York Times* writer David Brooks recently wrote an essay in *The Atlantic* theorizing that the nuclear family is obsolete. He points out that the image of the halcyon days' 1950 dinner table families we mythologize is actually a fantasy that was nothing more than an anomalous blip, and which needs to be retired in favor of something grander and more inclusive to a greater number of people. He discusses in the same essay how the forces that have steadily dismantled the larger, extended families of the first half of the 20th century (multiple generations living under one roof, and brothers and sisters living close by with their own families) have moved on to chip away at the nuclear family unit, breaking it down to single-parent homes.

"We're likely living through the most rapid change in family structure in human history. The causes are economic, cultural, and institutional all at once," Brooks writes. He later concludes: "It's time to find ways to bring back the big tables," referring to construction of a new family not restricted to biology, reminiscent of the utopian dream peddled in books like Hillary Clinton's seminal 1996 bestseller, *It Takes a Village*.

Brooks's thinking might be summarized as "Blood might make you related, but loyalty makes you family." Yet I believe replacing blood families with something else will be a trickier project than Brooks and Clinton imagine. Whatever shape larger, extended "families" of the future take, I do not believe we will get there without a healthier nuclear family. If there is one thing Brooks and I agree on, it is that the skeletal, single-parent grouping America is moving toward is not going to bring us to the promised village. After all, when a child loses a father, they lose a whole village of people who love them: aunts, uncles, cousins, grandmas, and grandpas.

While Brooks does not frame his ideas in feminism, antipathy toward the family unit is elemental to Third and Fourth Wave feminists; the dismantling of the family unit is a stated goal in much of their foundational literature. Brooks's essay is just more evidence of how pervasive the concept has become within the mainstream. It is beyond the scope of my expertise and the objective of this book to explore decades of feminist theory, but as best as I can surmise, the root of much modern feminist thinking contains the idea that the "traditional" family is an outdated, sexist vessel that perpetuates the parochial, patriarchal oppression of women.

The Village is on Fire

This trend is, in my opinion, dangerous to our social foundation, and yet unavoidable in today's world. A simple scan of the prevailing news— pre-COVID-19—confronts one with the blunt fact that the pendulum has lately swung from the Gillian Flynn brand of fantastically complex women deliciously victimizing others to a #MeToo era of fiction where female protagonists live in horrific patriarchies dominated by terrible men. Leni Zemas's *Red Clocks* and Christina Dalcher's *Vox* are just two examples of this feminist dystopia. In the latter, women receive electric shocks through bracelets if they dare utter more than one hundred words a day. Arguably, the recent TV adaptation of *The Handmaid's Tale* helped kick off this new trend, and of course

Margaret Atwood just released a sequel. Another book in this genre, which was much heralded at the beginning of 2019, *The Water Cure*, was described recently in *The New Yorker:*[23]

Three young sisters live with their parents in a decommissioned seaside sanatorium that was once a grand hotel. They have no contact with the outside; their father, King, leaves in a motorboat every few months to bring back supplies from a mainland they believe to be dangerously contaminated. Men are the primary source of the toxins, and the two elder sisters can remember when their parents provided a sanctuary for "damaged women," refugees who had been harmed by the male world.

Alas, a descent into the realm of fantasy is unnecessary to find the fairer female fable—it is alive and well in the stories told in the real world. Intimate partner violence is, for example, a societal ill that can have horrific consequences. Thankfully, abhorrence of spousal and child abuse is now central to Western morality, and we have developed strong legal mechanisms that provide the necessary latitude to protect women from dangerous men and children from dangerous parents. As a result, domestic violence rates have been declining for decades. In the US, rates of serious intimate partner violence against women fell by 72 percent between 1994 and 2011.

I have noted previously that men are undeniably more physically violent than women overall, making up as much as 80 percent of all convicted violent criminals in America.[24] However, the dynamics of intimate partner and family violence are as surprising as they are sensitive. For instance, the National Violence Against Women Survey found that among Respondents reporting intimate partner

23   Laura Miller, "A Twisted Fairy Tale About Toxic Masculinity," *New Yorker*, December 31, 2018, https://newyorker.com/magazine/2019/01/07/a-twisted-fairy-tale-about-toxic-masculinity

24   "Sex differences in crime," Wikipedia, last edited 6 August, 2020, https://en.wikipedia.org/wiki/Sex_differences_in_crime

violence in the last year, the ratio between women and men was 3:2.[25]

Since 1975, the National Family Violence Survey from the Family Research Laboratory at the University of New Hampshire has found that women are just as likely as men to report physically assaulting their spouse, and men just as likely to report being assaulted.[26] Findings like these have been confirmed by more than two hundred studies of intimate violence.[27]

Other data indicate that women are as likely as men to introduce violence into a relationship. For example, recent surveys at the CDC have found that an equal percentage of men and women reported being the victim of partner violence in the past year,[28] and that unidirectional violence is directed at men 70 percent of the time.[29]

In today's social climate, many readers will find this relative symmetry so counterintuitive as to be unbelievable. The sociological reasons why these numbers are difficult to contend with is beyond the scope of this discussion, but my purpose is to highlight the disparity in thinking and, in the process, emphasize that the emotional plight of men is underreported and underappreciated. That is not to dismiss the genuine struggles women confront, but rather to encourage readers to open their minds and consider the other half of the gender

---

25   Patricia Tjaden and Nancy Thoennes, *Full Report of the Prevalence, Incidence, and Consequences of Violence Against Women*, (Washington: Department of Justice, November 2000). https://ncjrs.gov/pdffiles1/nij/183781.pdf
26   Cathy Young, "The Surprising Truth About Women and Violence," *Time*, June 25, 2014, https://time.com/2921491/hope-solo-women-violence
27   Martin S. Fiebert, "References Examining Assaults By Women On Their Spouses Or Male Partners: An Annotated Bibliography," California State University, last updated June 2012, https://web.csulb.edu/~mfiebert/assault.htm
28   M.J. Breiding, J. Chen, and M.C. Black. *Intimate Partner Violence in the United States—2010*. (Atlanta: National Center for Injury Prevention and Control, Centers for Disease Control and Prevention, 2014). https://cdc.gov/violenceprevention/pdf/cdc_nisvs_ipv_report_2013_v17_single_a.pdf
29   Daniel J. Whitaker, et al., "Differences in Frequency of Violence and Reported Injury Between Relationships With Reciprocal and Nonreciprocal Intimate Partner Violence," *American Journal of Public Health* 97, no. 5 (May 1, 2007): 941-947. https://doi.org/10.2105/AJPH.2005.079020

paradigm—men suffer, too.

The blizzard of depressing data should not dissuade us from pressing for reform, however. I am hopeful of the future. But from where I stand, nothing remains surprising. Perhaps this will go some way in ameliorating any cognitive dissonance you might experience. While men are much more violent (and tend to cause greater injury in violent encounters due to greater strength, size, and other factors), the vast majority of male violence is inflicted on other men, often in the service of protecting women and children. This is what the average man's biological nature calls for.

According to the numbers, the safest living arrangement for a Western mother and her children involves a home with the biological father.[30] The fact is, the more social scientists study intimate partner violence, the clearer it becomes that it is best tackled as a human problem, rather than a gender one.

Just as we are reluctant to imagine women as criminals, we can't stomach meting out the justice deserved when they are actually convicted of crimes. Study after study definitively shows that women get more lenient sentences for just about every type of crime, with every variable accounted for. One study from 2012 found that in federal criminal cases, "men receive 63 percent longer sentences on average than women" and "[w]omen are . . . twice as likely to avoid incarceration if convicted." This makes the criminal sentencing gender gap six times as large as the racial disparity we hear so much about.[31]

---

30   "Child Abuse And Father Figures: Which Kind Of Families Are Safest To Grow Up In?" American SPCC, published August 16, 2017, https://americanspcc. org/2017/08/16/child-abuse-father-figures-kind-families-safest-grow

31   "Study Finds Large Gender Disparities In Federal Criminal Cases," University of Michigan, published November 16, 2012, http://law.umich.edu/ newsandinfo/features/Pages/starr_gender_disparities.aspx?fbclid=IwAR0iO sy0WBDTG481ggOoV5tIy8yugIzC5ARyaODmidhlyew6IUiaufljY5g

A War Between the Sexes is a Battle to the Bottom

These numbers make clear that there is an ongoing war between the sexes. That war is, in its existing construct, the very zero-sum game that I so desperately wanted to avoid in my efforts to broker reason and compromise with Dana. I briefly mentioned empathy in the last chapter; as a society, it is a deeply held belief that women are more empathetic than men. And perhaps it is true that they are, but not by much. A recent study of a large sample of American men and women found that if you take a random sampling of one man and one woman, the man would be more empathetic about one out of every three times.[32] That's fewer empathic women and more empathic men than one might expect in the reality we are regularly led to believe.

Gender myths extend into parenting, too. One established myth in Western culture claims that part of the reason fathers are worse parents is because we are emotionally crippled and urge our boys to suppress sadness and share their anger in its stead. However, a recent study found that both mothers and fathers felt it was more acceptable for their girls to express sadness *and* anger than it was for their boys.[33] Even further, it turned out that fathers didn't show any bias in their parenting methods between boys and girls—but mothers did.

In psychology, there might be no area of knowledge more universally accepted than the statistical trends established in the study of trait theory. Human personality can be broken down into clusters of traits that group together into the Big Five: openness, conscientiousness, extraversion, agreeableness, and neuroticism. How each of us scores in these five clusters on personality surveys provides deeper insight into our personality. Fascinatingly, differences between the personalities of

---

32   D.B.Wright, E.M.Skagerberg "Measuring Empathizing and Systemizing with a Large US Sample" *PLOS ONE* 7 no.2 (2012). https://doi.org/10.1371/journal.pone.0031661

33   Jen Monnier, "Moms Show Gender Bias Against Emotional Expression in Boys. But Why?" *Fatherly*, Jan 10 2020, https://www.fatherly.com/health-science/moms-gender-bias-boys-emotions

men and women have emerged around the world and across cultures. The most prominent Big Five finding is that women consistently show more neuroticism. Women who score high in neuroticism are more emotionally reactive and vulnerable to stress; they are more likely to experience everyday situations as threatening, and commonplace frustrations as hopelessly difficult.

My focus on men is not to suggest that I am blind to the problems from which women uniquely suffer. Women experience anxiety and depression at almost double the rates of men, for example. Author Andrea Petersen writes in his book about anxiety, *On Edge*, "There is no greater risk factor for anxiety disorders than being born female . . . women are about twice as likely as men to develop one, and women's illnesses generally last longer, have more severe symptoms, and are more disabling."[34] Of course, mental illness of any kind needs to be treated with empathy and professional understanding, but when it comes to the mental illness of women, we are much more reluctant to focus on how such psychological problems affect the circle of friends and loved ones around them, whereas this is often the central discussion when it comes to male illness. That focus ignores the fact that studies show that anxiety is not only partly biologically inherited, but also "contagious," in the sense that children pick it up from the mood created by the adults around them.[35]

Nor is the ultimate act of marital sabotage—infidelity—the exclusive domain of men. It is, in fact, an equal opportunity sport, though subject to the vicissitudes of gender peculiarities. Men cheat a little more in their younger years, for example, but the difference only becomes appreciable as men age into their 40s.[36]

---

34   Andrea Peterson, *On Edge* (Manhattan: Crown Publishing, 2017)
35   Kate Julian, "What Happened to American Childhood?" *The Atlantic*, April 17, 2020, https://www.theatlantic.com/magazine/archive/2020/05/childhood-in-an-anxious-age/609079
36   Wendy Wang, "Who Cheats More? The Demographics of Infidelity in America," Institute for Family Studies, January, 2018, https://ifstudies.org/blog/who-cheats-more-the-demographics-of-cheating-in-america

Many studies show that, while men are more dishonest overall, the difference is just a few percentage points in most instances, and sometimes it is a tie. In one study, when participants were asked if it was acceptable to steal from work if the person is experiencing financial trouble, 26 percent of women and 32 percent of men said yes. But when asked if it was acceptable to cross the street at a red light with no cars in sight, men and women endorsed the behavior at virtually the same level.[37] This stark reality does nothing to stem the growing excesses of the #MeToo movement, nor does it keep at bay the blind adherents to the #MeToo faith who swarm anyone who suggests that the #believewomen trend endangers the nation's foundational guarantee of due process and fair justice.

I acknowledge that the reasons we tend to fall into the fairer female fantasy are infinitely complicated, and the psychological underpinnings of an entire multi-millennia-old cultural tradition are beyond the scope of this book. In a longer conversation, I would agree that there are some benefits to society believing women are fairer. One of many reasons is that—due to biological realities that can't simply be re-engineered (hard as progressives may try)—women give birth to and are more suited to care for our children. I, like many men I know, often instinctually gravitate to gallantry, and sense that it is deeply written in our DNA to protect the most vulnerable among us—even if we sometimes mess up.

Much like the myth of the fairer sex, with just a cursory examination of real data, the idea of a society-wide oppression of women by a Western world patriarchy dissolves like the credibility of the Chinese Communist government in the midst of a pandemic.

The truth is, society has evolved dramatically and for the better with respect to equality of the sexes in a relatively short period of time. Examples of the positive trajectory of women abound—numbers we can all cheer about. There is growing gender symmetry in family

---

37   Ilona Jerabek, "The Subjectivity Of Honesty: New Study Reveals Gender Differences In Views of Dishonesty," *Cision*, June 17, 2017, https://prweb.com/releases/2017/06/prweb14410566.htm

finances, and in the US, 57 percent of women now participate in the workforce, compared with 69 percent of men.[38] Today, more than 66 percent of US families are dual income,[39] and the woman makes more money than her spouse in 37 percent of families.[40] Additionally, proper scrutiny of the wage gap shows that it has closed to the point of negligence, a claim which roils some critics—but the numbers don't lie. When all variables are accounted for, most credible experts place the gap at less than 5 percent.[41] Recent studies show that women make more than men before the age of thirty, like this one in the UK.[42]

None of this is to suggest that there is not more work to be done. There are several high-prestige careers dominated by men, including those in politics and finance. The C-suites of corporate America are still unbalanced, and maternity leave rules are still gravely subpar, but things are changing. Not to mention other male-dominated professions, like construction and sanitation, toward which women rarely scramble.

Regardless of the imbalances, we are veering into dangerous territory where female dysfunction and antisocial behavior is practically encouraged in all sorts of arenas, often justified with loquacious arguments that really don't boil down to anything more compelling than revenge fantasies; men deserve their just deserts

---

38   A.W. Geiger and Kim Parker, "Gender Gains—and Gaps—in the U.S," Pew Research Center, March 15, 2018, https://pewresearch.org/fact-tank/2018/03/15/for-womens-history-month-a-look-at-gender-gains-and-gaps-in-the-u-s
39   Gretchen Livingston and Kim Parker, "8 facts about American dads," Pew Research Center, June 12, 2019, https://pewresearch.org/fact-tank/2019/06/12/fathers-day-facts
40   R29 Brand Experiences, "What The Modern American Family Looks Like —By The Numbers," *Refinery*, 29 January 17, 2018, https://refinery29.com/en-us/women-breadwinners-household-income-family-impact
41   Stephen J. Dubner, "The True Story of the Gender Pay Gap," *Freakonomics*, January 7, 2016, https://freakonomics.com/podcast/the-true-story-of-the-gender-pay-gap-a-new-freakonomics-radio-podcast
42   Press Association, "Women in their 20s earn more than men of same age, study finds," *The Guardian*, August 29, 2015, https://theguardian.com/money/2015/aug/29/women-in-20s-earn-more-men-same-age-study-finds

for being horrible since time *ad infinitem*. It seems to me that the most ardent gender warriors have been forced into fancy footwork in order to dance around the empirical evidence piling up all around them and maintain the delusional view of a world scorched by the scourge of toxic masculinity.

Presenting evidence of women behaving badly might smack of something akin to the negative mudslinging of the very sort I am admonishing. That is not my intention. It's simply that alarm bells continually go off in my head as I walk through a cultural minefield saturated with commentary, entertainment, and academic work offering skewed thinking and terribly divisive ideas to an impressionable populace. Instead of examining how women can synthesize the best of masculinity, many commentators seem intent on shoveling up the violent, putrid sludge that represents the worst of humanity and rebranding it as strength and empowerment.

When we live in a world with statistics as horrific as this—where mothers kill their children at about the same rate as fathers—is it not high time we pull the curtain back on the charade?[43] Can we push *pause* and break down the twin illusions of male defectiveness and female exceptionalism? Can we not adopt a more humanist, less confrontational approach to bettering society? Can we choke out toxicity and dysfunction, whomever it may come from, and supply more oxygen to the complementary strengths of femininity and masculinity?

Let's Pedestalize the Patriarch

These illusions and their implications are destructive precisely because most of the focus of parenting falls to the pure magic of motherhood—with good reason. Biology dictates that a mother is most important for the beginnings of life, because infants are

---

43   Bourget, "A Review of Maternal and Paternal Filicide," 74-82. http://jaapl.org/content/jaapl/35/1/74.full.pdf

dependent on their mother for survival. You would be hard-pressed to find a man who denies that there is nothing more bewitchingly beautiful and profound than pregnancy and childbirth. The evolution of a woman as she carries a child and brings them into the world is enchanting and miraculous. Many fathers understand how foundational the matriarch is to being a human and are greatly moved by the mystery and magic of it all.

Focus on the mother, however, often means fathers are left out.

"We tend to put mothers on a pedestal, quite rightly," says Dr. Anna Machin, an Oxford anthropologist who is one of the few academics studying fathers. "But dad is left on the floor, labelled as either absent or inept. I think we need to balance that negative story with the positive."

As Dr. Machin and other researchers turn their attention to fathers, they have discovered that men go through physiological and psychological changes right along with the mother in preparation for a baby's birth. Our hormones shift and our brains physically change. Just like the mother, our minds and bodies get ready for the deep bond that comes with the early years of fathering. As time goes by, though, we must move toward a more grown-up, disinterested love of our children.

"Fathers build profound attachments with their children," Machin says—but the bonds are slightly different and grow largely from interaction and rough-and-tumble play. Men nurture their children by providing more challenge: "[Dad's] job is to challenge. To be the secure base from which the child goes out into the world to investigate what is going on. His role is to teach the skills— behavioral, linguistic, cognitive—that will enable that child to deal with life's challenges, assess its risks and leap over those hurdles."

Children without fathers are more likely to experience worse outcomes in just about every conceivable metric—the evidence is indisputable. It is also established science that a poorly managed divorce, particularly one that includes the loss of a loving parent, is a source of deep childhood trauma. And now there is a growing body of evidence that adults with traumatic love-starved childhoods become more susceptible to nearly every psychological and physical illness there is.

"Trauma's fingers reach deep into every part of the body and mind," writes Jade Wu, a Ph.D. in Psychology and columnist for *Psychology Today*. Not only can childhood trauma cause physical illness, but it can cause lifelong problems in trusting others, in establishing a stable identity, and it can even distort memory and the ability to plan. The implications are clear: bad divorces create sicker children.

Fathers must step into this reality. No matter what the culture at large wants us to believe, we are essential to our children. We must wrest back the crown of fatherhood, polish its tarnished reputation, and wear it nobly. In 2000, United States Supreme Court Justice and feminist icon Ruth Bader Ginsburg famously exclaimed, "Women will only have true equality when men share with them the responsibility of bringing up the next generation." Today, fathers like me, so eager to be a part of their children's lives, understand that not only have swaths of policymakers and perception-empowerers ignored Ginsburg's entreaty, but also that our foundational legal institutions actively work against fathers as they fight to maintain their rightful place in the family.

"Many fathers come up against quite considerable cultural and societal barriers in being involved fathers," says Dr. Machin. "It is very true when we say it takes a whole village to raise a child, but let's just remember that right at the center of that village is dad."

I am not, to reiterate, nostalgically pining for a return to female subjugation. I have already conceded that the nuclear family was long overdue for serious reform by the middle of last century—but the crack in this theory is the same that runs through any dogma that reduces human relations to a battle between two opposing groups. I would argue it is exactly this kind of one-dimensional thinking that has driven us to create legally binding power differentials in family law, and to build a divorce industry with this binary thinking at its core.

Every marriage partner or ex-partner at some point learns that keeping score in a relationship and tabulating who is gaining and who is losing—as opposed to concentrating on whether the boat of the entire family is rising—ends with everyone drowning. If we are going to get to a better place, we have to discard our crude existential choices and refocus our energies on creating the magic that can only result when men and women work as a complementary team, negotiating and working through their differences as mature, secure, functioning adults. This may seem a little utopian; I'll admit, keeping score sounds like a human characteristic, one not necessarily wedded—no pun intended—to marriage. The question I derive from this discussion is how marriage as an institution can mediate our national and often destructive instincts in service of the interests of the marital unit (and, by extension, society). It cannot neuter or eliminate those instincts—no human institution can—but can it temper them better than is presently the case? Because in its current construct, as I seem to see it, marriage inflames our worst passions, rather than soothing them.

I believe we must transition to reconciliation and cooperation, because the post-divorce reality for the vast majority of families simply doesn't resemble the hundreds of TV shows, books, and films that depict divorce for laughs and light drama. In real life, there are no montages of dad and the kids painting the new apartment, joyous smiles plastered on their faces; there is no celebrity "conscious decoupling" or first-class continent-hopping for the kids. Satisfaction and closure are, for the most part, the domain of Hollywood's candy-floss confection machine. For those of us experiencing the harsh realities of divorce, it frequently takes the form of our very own endless, dreary British football game—we live in an unsatisfying nil-nil draw while the kids slump in the stands in the rain.

CHAPTER 14

SPIRIT LEVEL
OF THE (S)EXES

"Faith and Belief can be a most dogged pallbearer"

Augustine of Hippo was a North African philosopher and theologian known for his contribution to the Just War theory, a doctrine positing that violence might be morally justified only as a last resort to right a grave wrong—it must not be pre-emptive and aggressive, only defensive. Family law in America has no regard for Just War theory. It does not favor moral conduct. To the contrary, it promotes a first-strike offensive, urges a shock ambush and power grab, favors the ruthless, and rewards the unethical.

Men with stories like mine are legion—men who have become reluctant participants in an adversarial system of uncivil war we did not start and are utterly powerless to stop. As we jump through the legal hoops like good dogs, we are gutted outside the courtroom: ghosted by friends, excommunicated from our community, blackballed and blackmailed by unqualified, unscrupulous visitation monitors and child services ideologues, plagued by parasitical "legal experts," and psyched out by pseudo-intellectual psychiatrists. And inside the courtroom is worse.

None of this is strictly a product of social prejudices. There is money at stake, and American divorce is big business, raking in more than $60 billion a year by some estimates. At the core of the industrial complex are the courts, supplemented by all the supporting bureaucracies, businesses, enforcement agencies, lawyers, private investigators, social workers, child meeting monitors, mediators, psychotherapists, child support agents, guardians *ad litem*, police officers, and judges. How did we get here?

The No-Fault Fallacy

Among the primary culprits is the existing structure of purported no-fault divorce law, a by-product of the rapid expansion of divorce in the 1970s and 1980s. No-fault divorce laws took the country by storm during that period, and an entire parasitic industry evolved in the process. Many people are under the illusion that no-fault divorce involves two adults mutually consenting to dissolve a marriage without placing any blame. Indeed, the idea of no-fault divorce was to render the process less onerous and intrusive, especially for women, and the system might even achieve this for a soon-to-be-ex-couple who agrees on a calm and equitable way forward.

But no-fault divorce laws are egregiously misnamed, because in cases where the spouses hold diverging views on whether or not the split should happen, how it should happen, and what the post-split future should look like, the system invokes an entire infrastructure of presumptive fault—and much more than before no-fault laws were written. These laws, as currently enforced, typically allow for a unilateral decision by one spouse to dissolve a marriage without any particular wrongdoing by the other spouse. In fact, no-fault divorce renders the idea of marriage as a binding agreement mostly an illusion. In other areas of contract law, if you break a contract for no reason, you are expected to compensate your ex-partner. In breaking a marriage contract for no reason, however, the outcome is most often exactly the reverse, thus setting the stage for a whole universe of bad behavior.

I am not advocating a return to the days when a woman trapped in an unhappy marriage would need to prove her right to dissolve the union. We have moved past that undeniably prejudicial construct. Rather, I merely advocate the no-fault laws embody what they purport to represent—that is, a system that allows for the dissolution of a marriage without any presumptions of fault. I advocate this with such passion precisely because these laws as practiced, if not as intended, are riven with assumptions of male perniciousness and malice that lays waste to their no-fault premise.

There are, as ever, defenders of the status quo. Many in the system will tell you that the Petitioner more often wins custody of the kids and the bulk of the assets, but there are no reliable national numbers. Even so, many states' statistics hint at the issue. In the state of Wisconsin, for example, the number of fathers awarded sole custody of their children decreased from 11 percent in 1988 to 9 percent in 2008,[44] despite all of the shifts in society I have outlined—more mothers in the workforce and fathers doing a greater portion of parenting. Given women are the Petitioner up to 90 percent of the time in family court cases, you can piece the reality together. My case certainly followed that pattern. It felt to me—and this seems consistent with the system as a whole—as if the courts determined a need to reward the parent who brings in the business with a finder's fee. And today that reward is most often slid into the palm of a woman.

Historically, before no-fault laws, the narrative held that it was an unscrupulous cheating man who abandoned his family to ride off into the sunset with a new belle. But the story today is often this: a slightly unhappy woman gets a Plan B man set up outside the marriage under a hardworking man's nose, then rides off into the sunset with the kids and half his money.

"It's a game of what we in political science call a prisoner's dilemma, whoever betrays the other first wins," says Stephen Baskerville, Ph.D., author of many books on divorce and the dynamics between the sexes

44   Maria Cancian et al, "Who Gets Custody Now? Dramatic Changes in Children's Living Arrangements After Divorce," *Demography* 51, (2014): 1381–1396, https://doi.org/10.1007/s13524-014-0307-8

and their impact on society, and former president of the American Coalition for Fathers and Children. "It's also known as the race to the courthouse."[45]

Once the Petitioner ventures into the multilayered family law ecosystem, arcane processes whir to life to assign blame, divvy up the spoils, and pull the kids from the Respondent in an awesome show of authoritarian force by the state.

"The family courts are the most intrusive, the most invasive government machinery that has ever existed in English-speaking democracies," says Baskerville. "The violation of the privacy of the household and the privacy of the individual are just beyond belief and beyond anything else in our society. It involves violations of a person's constitutional rights on the most basic level."

Baskerville is not alone in his views. Countless experts in family law assert that no-fault divorce—which has existed in the US for fifty years—is, in fact, unconstitutional, and denies citizens the due process protections afforded them under the 5th and 14th Amendments. The guarantees of these two amendments are so central to American jurisprudence that their command is the only one found twice in the Constitution. The 5th Amendment says to the federal government that no one shall be "deprived of life, liberty or property without due process of law." The 14th Amendment uses the very same words to tell the states the same thing. Essentially, the two amendments together are an assurance that Americans will never be jailed without a fair trial, that their property won't be confiscated and redistributed without a fair trial, and that their children's right to a parent won't be taken away indiscriminately and without fair procedures. But today's divorce courts routinely trample all over these rights through a combination of the states' relinquishment of the responsibility to assign legal culpability over the breaking of the marriage contract and the overzealous application of protection mechanisms in the name of abuse allegations that, in practice, are available for women only.

---

45   Stephen Baskerville, *Taken Into Custody: The War Against Fathers, Marriage, and the Family*, (2007)

"The fallout from no-fault divorce has thus been financially, emotionally and physically devastating to divorced families with increases in poverty, suicide, depression, drug and alcohol abuse and more," says Beverly Willett, co-founder of the Coalition for Divorce Reform.[46]

The Growing Support for a Repeal of No-Fault Divorce

Perhaps because of the developing recognition of the system's inherent prejudices, the most powerful and fundamental change to the system would be the repeal of no-fault laws across the nation. Despite being a bit of a pipe dream, the idea of rethinking the entire idea of no-fault divorce is gaining traction.

Like many people who take up this mantle, Willett is not only an advocate for change but also a casualty of divorce court in her own life. She points to how the specifics of these laws fly in the face of all other contract law, and are, in fact, unconstitutional. According to Willett, an explicit reminder of the protections legal marriage are meant to provide spouses and the ways in which no-fault divorce knee-caps these rights were provided during the Supreme Court battle to legalize same-sex marriage.

"These [no-fault] laws . . . transgress the Constitution's guarantee of substantive due process," Willett says. "In its decision legalizing same-sex marriage, the US Supreme Court reiterated the fundamental right to marriage and its sweeping benefits—everything from companionship and security to safeguarding children to tax, inheritance, health insurance and myriad other benefits. No-fault, however, renders these rights hollow. They must be forfeited without cause or compensation."

In a fascinating twist, same-sex marriages—or, I should say, same-sex divorces—just happen to provide helpful evidence of the gender bias in family court. When same-sex couples with children walk into

---

46   Beverly Willett, "What fifty years of no-fault divorce has gotten us," *Washington Examiner*, August 13, 2019,https://washingtonexaminer.com/opinion/op-eds/what-fifty-years-of-no-fault-divorce-has-gotten-us

divorce court, more often than not they walk out with shared parenting orders closer to 50/50 than do their heterosexual contemporaries.

The list of ways we could improve family law institutions are almost endless.

The Child Support "Cash Cow"

The no-fault fallacy is but one of the family law "reforms" that has devolved the system into its present moral and ethical quagmire. And nowhere is the pernicious force of this law of unintended consequences practiced more starkly than in the towering racket of our child support regime. Federal laws concerning child support were passed a few decades back, and if no-fault divorce keeps lawyers' billable hour meters ticking, then the child support system keeps county coffers overflowing.

In the final episode of season three of *Westworld*, an omniscient, faceless Artificial Intelligence machine that spun out of control and manipulates humans to turn on each other says: "Every human relationship can be adjusted with the right amount of money." That should be carved into the cold stone at the entrance to every divorce court. Money is at the root of all its berserk evils.

The child support system we have now grew out of a federal law called Title IV-D, created in the '70s to help keep the welfare system solvent. Back then, men were the breadwinners in 80 percent of homes, and as the number of divorces exploded after no-fault laws swept the nation, a wave of women were forced into the welfare system after relationship breakdowns, especially in low-income families. It only made sense in this imbalanced employment dynamic to help mothers with little earning power through legal instruments that forced fathers to support children caught in the middle.

For the welfare system, these forced payments by the father offset the increases in welfare payout—at least in theory. The truth, however, is that the system was never all that successful at collecting money from low-income fathers, partly due to uninvolved fathers who desired to keep it that way, but often because the fathers didn't have much money.

Before long, classic mission creep set in and the laws initially designed to support welfare expanded to ensure the transfer of money from middle class fathers to middle class mothers, even while employment opportunities for women opened up and the financial imbalances between parents evaporated. With the middle class, municipalities found more success in collecting money.

If women are on their way to equal pay and if society is moving closer and closer to financial parity, then theoretically money does not need to change hands anymore, right? How does one keep the easy money coming? Manufacture a new imbalance by ensuring that the mother of the divorce is given threefold more time with the kids than the father—effectively rendering the dad nothing more than an outcast, a family scapegoat who gets the right to "visit" his kids four days a month only if he compensates for the mother's other twenty-six days of extra parenting time that he has been denied. In America, the standard post-divorce parenting schedule makes the father an every-second-weekend visitor.

The scam gets even better; the county collects the money from one parent and disburses it to the other, effectively making themselves the middleman. This money is most often separate from state budgets. And here is the kicker: the amount of federal subsidies dispersed to counties and states are tied to the amount of child support money they haul in! The states and counties have a clear financial incentive not only to create broken homes, but to ensure the parenting schedule is as lopsided as possible. The greater the parenting time differential, the higher the child support payments moving through the system, and thus the bigger the subsidy checks from the Feds.

Child support money is the cash cow of the county judiciaries, making up some 35 percent to half of civil litigation. Men are ordered to pay support in 85 percent of cases even though women now make more money than men 41 percent of the time.[47] The monthly payments are tax-free and often garnished directly from the father's paycheck. And when mothers are ordered to pay child support, they fail to do so more often than men.[48]

Dead Broke Dads

The idea of the deadbeat dad from yesteryear is largely a myth now, kept alive by people with an agenda. There are exceptions, of course. These outliers remind me of a scene from the movie *Fight Club*:

> Ed Norton: "I don't know my dad. I mean, I know him, but he left when I was six years old. Married this other woman and had a bunch of kids. And he did this every six years. Goes to a new city and starts a new family."

> Brad Pitt: "Fucker's setting up franchises."

Studies show that most men who fail to pay child support are not like those populating pop culture—anti-Daddy-Warbuckses hiding money in numbered bank accounts in the Cayman Islands. Rather, most are simply men doing their best, and have often gone broke because the amount they are being asked to pay is unnecessarily inflated.

So profound is the punitive effect of these forces that for some men, not paying child support involves jail—with no trial. Stories of men destroyed by the cycle in the system are endless, and thousands of these tales go the same way: a woman wants to leave her marriage but can't afford it. Out of the blue, she claims abuse, and a man with no history of legal trouble is kicked out of his home, loses his kids and half his life's spoils, and is ordered to pay more than he can afford in monthly child

---

47   Nathan Arnold, "Dads Represent 85% Of Child Support Providers, Pay More Than Female Payers," *Dads Divorce*, 2018, https://dadsdivorce.com/articles/dads-represent-85-of-child-support-providers-pay-more-than-female-payers
48   Rachel Martin, "Who Fails To Pay Child Support? Moms, At A Higher Rate Than Dads," *NPR*, March 1, 2015, https://www.npr.org/2015/03/01/389945311/who-fails-to-pay-child-support-moms-at-a-higher-rate-than-dads

support. The connection to everything he loves and knows severed, he falls into depression and loses his job. He can't pay child support without the job and is thrown in jail—a life-changing experience that further undermines his mental health, the trauma exacerbating his PTSD. While he is in jail, the unpaid monthly payments stack up—yes, the financial burden is not suspended even when he has no possible way to earn an income—and he leaves jail with a criminal record, a growing mountain of unpaid child support, and no home to live in (that privilege having been extended to his ex-wife and kids, perhaps even with a new man). There is no welfare money for him, only insurmountable debt he must work multiple jobs to afford, all while he tries to manage his psychological pain. This sort of downward spiral can sputter to a horrific end in just a matter of months.

To many who have studied the policies at the heart of this dynamic, the whole thing is a grift, a brazen racket.

"This is a legal underworld. Some people have described it as a system of organized crime, and that's really what it is," says Baskerville. This cartel of family law war is culling our communities, killing our children, murdering our families, all under the cloak (and dagger) of legal integrity.

The Inconvenient Elegance of Shared Parenting

One legislative solution to the dilemma of separate parents is the legal concept of an equal, shared parenting presumption, or a rebuttable 50/50 parenting presumption, for parenting time, legal custody, and physical custody. While some states use slightly different terminology, these areas are all part of the litigation that benefit the divorce industry at the expense of children. Under these laws, a divorce would start with the default presumption that what is in the best interest of the children is for both parents to equally share in the parenting. Under this paradigm, it becomes incumbent upon the petitioning lawyer and the judge to provide more comprehensive explanations for any deviations from this baseline of equal parenting, circumscribing some of the state's freedom to make arbitrary assessments about which parent is "better" or "fitter" than the other and making it more onerous to justify any other outcome than a 50/50 time split.

Many advocacy groups have worked tirelessly for years in an effort to advance this conceptual framework. One such organization, founded by fearless family advocate Molly K. Olson in 2013, is Leading Women for Shared Parenting. Their statement on divorce and parenting reads, in part: "Parental separation should not spell the end of a relationship between a child and one of its parents. Forced separation from one's own flesh and blood in the absence of abuse is morally wrong and socially irresponsible."[49] During the drive to get a shared parenting bill passed into law in Minnesota, Senator Karin Housley said, "There is nothing more sacred than the parent-child relationship. This bill is to protect children who have loving, responsible parents who are ready, willing and able to share equally in the responsibility of raising them." Senator Housley heroically got the bill through her Senate Family Care and Aging Committee and it passed unanimously. But the Senate bill was required to go through one more committee, the MN Senate Judiciary Committee, and the chair of that committee refused to hear it so the bill never went to the Senate floor for a vote.

Could shared parenting sweep the nation like no-fault divorce did in the '70s? More than half of the states have introduced shared parenting bills in the last four years. As of this writing, Alabama, Kentucky, Missouri, Oregon, and Virginia have passed some level of shared parenting legislation into law, although some are more robust than others, none are adequate and most are quickly usurped by the family law firms who find slick ways to (mis)interpret the laws in their favor.

In 2012 in Arizona, grassroots advocates got language into their statute stating "the courts shall maximize parenting time." This was seen as a big development at the time, because the law was buttressed with judicial training provided by Arizona State University Professor

---

49   http://lw4sp.org

Dr. William Fabricius. He educated judges on the volumes of social science research which clearly states children do best when they maximize time with each parent. However, since then, the divorce lawyers figured out a way to circumvent this bill, as it was never defined in law what "maximize" even means. The term actually has no teeth unless specifically defined in law, so the divorce lawyers in Arizona merely drag out the legal battles before the case goes to court to avoid any perception that equal parenting is a standard. Additionally, Arizona has not changed their parenting time guide produced by the courts that restricts a father's custody to every other weekend, so the Arizona court guide does not accurately reflect equal parenting presumption at all.

In Nevada, equal parenting is a "preference" (not a mandate) for cases where parents agree. And wherever shared parenting bills are introduced in any state, there are always two groups that show up at the state houses to fight the proposals: divorce lawyer lobbies and feminist organizations. Not "equality" feminists like Camille Paglia or Christina Hoff Sommers, but a misandrist strain of radical feminists who infiltrate the domestic violence groups for added "cover" to perpetuate the myth that all women are poor helpless victims and all men are "potential" DV batterers and perpetrators. With groups of women like this opposing equal parenting bills, it's as if their Minority Report agenda is to punish men for "pre-crimes."

Kentucky and Arkansas are the only two states with clear statutory guidance favoring equally shared parenting. Both states also provide protections for victims of domestic violence. Ongoing legislative enhancements will balance those protections with the need to address concerns around false allegations employed as a tactic to thwart shared parenting.

In 2018, Kentucky was the first state to pass a law for a clear rebuttable presumption of equal shared parenting time. A few other considerations were added to their law. They included a special exception for domestic violence. State court data indicates domestic violence has gone down since equal parenting was passed. In 2021, Arkansas became the second state with a clear presumption of equal parenting time. They are the first state to include the evidentiary standard "clear and convincing evidence," which is the correct standard when implicating a fundamental right. Arkansas included an exception for the age of the child. Credible peer-reviewed social science research doesn't support less time for dads based on age of the child.

Every statutory scheme and definitions are different, so state laws for equal parenting time and custody will always vary and can't be replicated exactly, even when trying to achieve the same policy. Individual legislators often succumb to misinformation or a need to appease opponents which can lead to special bill language and exceptions that waters down the policy. There's an old family law axiom: "who controls the definitions, controls the outcomes." Legislators should know and follow the key principles needed to ensure effective equal shared parenting statutes. The laws passed are so broad they still allow for far too may false allegations of domestic violence. Isn't it time false allegations of domestic violence be considered a crime with statutory consequences? Elsewhere in law, in most states, it is a crime to make a false police report, so shouldn't it be the same with false allegations of domestic violence? If allegations of DV were tried in criminal (not civil) court, it might deter more false accusations, ensure more consequences, and have the added benefit of holding those who actually do commit acts of violence, domestic or otherwise, to be held more accountable.

I tend not to mistake law for justice. Justice is an ideal, and law is a tool. I think it's high time we improve the tool of law so that judges will be better equipped to administer justice in a more equitable manner.

Educating Judges

We need judges who are better educated on the social and psychological forces at work in their courtrooms. How do the people presiding over civil proceedings have the power to immediately and irreparably sever the bond between parent and child, permanently rupturing a family unit, even without secondary expertise in child psychology and family dynamics?

The legal precepts and instruments at the core of family law are not overly complicated, even shrouded as they are in arcane jargon. Years of toiling in the legal mechanics of carving up bank accounts and officiating he-said/she-said squabbles simply does not and cannot make a judge an expert in the complicated and notoriously counterintuitive area of family dysfunction, parental alienation, and child psychology. But such is not the case with matters of the mind, where what appears to be one thing is very often something else entirely—particularly where children are concerned—and the truth may only be visible to the properly trained eye.

We can't expect judges to become child psychologists simply because they serve a stint in the family courts before moving on to other assignments, but we can and must demand that they be better informed of the stark forces at work outside their courtrooms which inform what happens within them. I have, in these pages, ticked off myriad statistics pointing to the basic fact that neither men nor women wear the white hat in this corrosive battle of the sexes, and that women are every bit as likely to turn a venomous gaze on men as the other way around. Beyond that, other particularly pernicious phenomena, such as parental alienation and its effect on children of divorcing parents, are national tragedies unfolding in American courtrooms everyday, but with little or no judicial recognition.

Some would say such an educational advancement is completely impractical. I would counter: why do we have some doctors that are general practitioners and others who train further to be heart surgeons? In the end, a family court judge should be either a heart surgeon in discharging his or her duties, or at least have a system in place where a heart surgeon is available to guide the court through the process of dismantling families and allocating rights over children. But neither is present now—judges instead preside over a veritable, neonatal-like hospital ward populated by vulnerable kids and "adults" feeling and acting their worst under the weight of obliterated dreams and unresolved grief.

Judges in family court need to start by adhering to their duty to protect individual rights of each person in the courtroom. Since the US Supreme Court has made it consistently clear over decades, there is a constitutionally protected fundamental right to the parent-child relationship. Family court judges must recognize they have a duty to protect the relationship, not a duty to decide which parent is better and marginalize the other.

At the very least, we know judges get a lot of training on domestic violence; and often that training is provided directly from domestic violence advocates. Judges should have at least equal training on the importance of both parents and the parenting arrangements social science has found to provide the best outcomes for kids. That training should come from the researchers themselves. Or perhaps divorce, along with the custody and parenting time battles, should be taken out of the courts entirely.

Better Training for Those Deep in the System

It is not just judges who could use more and better education and training. Police, child protection agency workers, and lawyers should be better trained in family dynamics and child psychology. For example, in California, monitors for supervised visitations do not need a license. They are trusted with analyzing the most intimate moments a parent is permitted with their children, and often with transporting these children to and from visitations, all with little to no training. The part-time, transient nature of the work often leaves you to deal with people from the bottom of the barrel.

Law enforcement officers on the front line need better procedural guidelines and training for domestic disturbances. If police show up to a dispute in which a parent with no past history of violence and no relevant criminal record is accused of abuse or threatened abuse, law enforcement must prioritize the legal rights of the accused over the accuser.

For some context, much-needed adjustments are being made to

the way colleges investigate sexual assault on American campuses. Changes brought to schools under Title IX requirements in the '90s resulted in the creation of clearly inadequate systems, with untrained school administrators serving as judge and jury, consistently trampling over accused students' constitutional right to due process. In the same way, family law is stuffed to the gills with ideologically possessed staffers making life-and-death choices about law and order for which they are completely unqualified. Not much in life has frightened me more than the psychotic Cheshire Cat smile of the social worker from the Los Angeles Department of Children and Family Services as she prowled the halls of the Stanley Mosk Courthouse. And so, imagine my shock when, as I entered the courtroom for a hugely important child custody hearing in 2018—three years after my first encounter with this social worker —I saw her and Dana inside the Courthouse child custody evaluation waiting room, intimately discussing my case. The social worker had left her position with the DCFS and had subsequently started working as a family court services specialist in the very department that would evaluate if and how much time I might legally be allowed to spend with my sons. Witnessing her with Dana before I was called to be evaluated by her colleague was yet another layer of insurmountable torment. Are there any rules in this system?

The Single-Parent Kafka Trap

The list of ways family court could be improved is almost endless. A deep dive into the minutiae of family court bureaucracy and legal instruments is my purview.

Mark Ludwig is an advocate who began working for change in family law after being blindsided by the system. His speech at a Pennsylvania House Judiciary Committee hearing distills the hypocrisy and inhumanity of family court down to its charcoal essence:

> Shortly after my son was born, I went two hundred and four days without seeing him. At the end of that time

I was relegated to the equivalent of an every-other-weekend visitor. Shortly after that, I was diagnosed with a large growth in my brain. We didn't know what my future was going to be like. And it dawned on me at that point: if something were to happen to me, my son's mum would automatically get sole custody. But it also dawned on me that if the situation had been reversed, I would have automatically gotten sole custody of the very son that I was already only getting every other weekend with. Why would it take the death of a parent to convert from an every-other-weekend visitor to having full custody of a child?

His was a question with no good answer. I am a father who hasn't seen his two boys for nearly two years and counting, and not a single day has gone by that I don't ask the same thing.

That sense of ongoing incarceration—from my career, from my home, from my boys—consumed me for months after March 5, 2015. The divorce and its scourge became my life, not merely a painful life event from which I could recover. I am certain that countless men, trapped in their own journey to nowhere, feel similar hopelessness and despair. I emerged, battered though unbowed, because I eventually realized my own reckoning was due. Not a reckoning of the system, or a contextualizing of its prejudices and punitive assumptions—though, as I hope this book makes clear, understanding the system is an essential part of recovering from the maelstrom (or *male*-strom) of divorce—but a personal reckoning, one in which I faced my own failings and misconduct and their contribution to everything that happened, both to me and because of me. That is not to fall on my dagger writ large—I did not deserve the fate handed to me on March 5. But only in facing that personal reckoning could I ultimately understand those events for which I was responsible, and those for which I was not. Although difficult, it was a mirror that I had to face.

FOLIES À DEUX

(A MADNESS SHARED BY TWO)

Filled up and fuelled by her mother's failings,
Flailing upwards,
Spiralling down to unfeeling mediocrity,
Unaware of insobriety, in society,
She weaves,
Waving flags of attack dogs into the savage fray.

The acceptor—delusionary receptive,
The primary—elusively deceptive,
Repeating maladies old and new,
Of a madness shared by two.

Cunning stunts,
Symptomatically devious fronts,
Wants ordered by the General,
With needy, greedy expedient weaponry,
Housed in hollowed-out war chests,
Melodious melancholic reactionary action-men,
Repeating maladies old and new,
Of a madness shared by two.

PART THREE

REDEMPTION

A PRINCE'S PRAYER
1968- ?

My hero's journey,
A thousand faces worn.
The dash between the dead and born.
Am I not lost without her?
Or found within me?
I forget her,
To remember myself.
Forever and ever.

-A Man

CHAPTER 15

MY OWN PROBLEM PERPETRATOR

"Tomorrow I vow to make better mistakes."

There's a mountain of cocaine on the table. I'm sitting on a low couch in an exclusive Hollywood after-hours club called The Mousetrap that looks no different than any unremarkable suburban bungalow. It's circa-2010 and the clock is chiming some ungodly hour—God only knows which one. Sitting beside me is a long-time friend, a household name actor whose seminal catchphrase is "Drinking is a goal-oriented endeavor." We were led here by a guy who looked like Huggie Bear from the '70s cop show *Starsky and Hutch*, passing Bob De Niro in reception, Harry Dean Stanton in the living room, and behind the bedroom doors it's all narcotics and sex.

I have a few tales that start like this one, having lived and worked as an actor in Los Angeles for more than twenty years with an ample amount of jet-setting. But it's not what you think—I hardly drink. As a relative teetotaler my whole life, I have played the role of trusty wingman and designated driver for more than one actor friend.

In my youth back in England, while my peers were coming of age, drinking and fighting in pubs, I was busy chasing girls.

Throughout my film career there were epic bouts of thespian carousing where the booze flowed like honey. The *Pirates of the Caribbean* productions come to mind. The first film was shot on the island of St. Vincent and the Grenadines. On days off, the principal actors would sit around playing poker and drinking rum. By the time of the fourth film in Hawaii, as a bit of a social butterfly, it often fell on me to invite cast and crew—including Ian McShane, Penelope Cruz, and Stephen Graham—to various gatherings, dinners, and parties on behalf of Jerry Bruckheimer. When the production moved to London a few months later, there would be dinners, then nightcaps in and around the Covent Garden Hotel with the likes of Geoffrey Rush, Kevin Bacon, Stephen Sondheim, and Ralph Fiennes.

But through it all, I managed to keep my head and keep the drinking to a minimum. A sip of beer here, a glass of wine there, but never anything too serious. Harder drugs were always on the menu. The first time I was offered cocaine was on the set of a little movie called *Titanic* circa 1996 while filming on location in Rosarito Beach in Mexico. I turned it down then, and a hundred subsequent times.

I know—that first paragraph seemed to announce a fun passage of Hollywood salaciousness and debauchery and I've left you hanging. But that lead-in makes what happened next so unexpected.

I stared at the mountain of coke. And then, after thirty years in show business, my curiosity finally got the better of me. I leaned into the mountain (which wasn't mine!) and gave it a very tentative go. Sixty seconds later, I was babbling incessantly about how it wasn't affecting me, although I felt like I was at the dentist, shot through with Novocain.

My experimentation with cocaine, though not habitual or consistent, continued sporadically until I flushed the speckled remnants of what I had down the toilet on March 5 of 2015, shortly before receiving that fateful knock on the door. I mention it, though, because it was among the symptoms of my emotional descent, and it is therefore relevant to the story in its entirety.

None of this was obvious to the world around me. A stranger would be forgiven for believing I was living the dream that night in 2010; my career was taking off and I was working tirelessly in TV and film, with countless voiceover jobs. But all of this meant Dana and I were spending less and less time together. She would be gone on business trips and I would be home with the kids. Then I would jet off to a film location for weeks, leaving her to tend to the household. She and I had forged a strange and efficient consensus—I would work, she would travel, and we would switch off taking the kids. We were a well-oiled marriage machine. And we were complete strangers. But it hadn't always been this way.

A Faustian Marriage Bargain

A decade earlier, Dana and I started out on our journey together in Los Angeles, where we had moved a year after our impulsive nuptials in that Vegas chapel. It was a small, humbling Hollywood beginning. We found a cramped apartment to rent near Olympic and La Brea. Dana was in substantial debt, but I had considerable savings and we started to live off the rental income generated from the house I had left behind in London. She eventually landed good work at a flagship Rodeo Drive store and steadily worked her way up the ranks. As for me, I learned that it mattered not what body of work I brought with me to America—Hollywood didn't care. After six months I secured an agent and embarked on the thankless and soul-crushing task of auditioning.

Dana did not ask me to deal with my psychological trauma, and I returned the favor. We were both damaged, but neither of us wanted to disrupt our permanent vacation from reality and tempt the other to confront and exorcise their demons. Instead, we pretended they did not exist.

Even so, our respective behavior patterns, rooted in our respective upbringings, were creeping to the surface and neither of us were able to help each other. Rather, we played into each other's pathologies, dancing together in a co-addicted love tango. Our communication deteriorated as we focused on our careers, for the most part uniting only to co-parent.

Secrets and Wives

The result was painfully isolating. Dana lost any capacity for affection and rarely offered comfort or physical intimacy. She was burrowed in her cocoon, and nothing could fracture the hard-shell exterior. Addicted to the validation that physical contact delivers—however fleeting and counterfeit it might be—I found comfort elsewhere. My first transgression occurred a mere eighteen months after our wedding day. There were more transgressions to come in the next eighteen years, and after each one I returned home and resumed my synthetic role as a devoted family man.

We agreed to an unspoken covenant, a conspiracy of silence, a gruesome, unsustainable Faustian bargain. She would quietly allow me unfettered discretion to do what I wanted without scrutiny, and I would permit her to cut off her emotional oxygen, and together we would ignore the darker realities that might intrude on our fantasy. We enveloped ourselves in a bubble of emotional anesthesia and amnesia.

Single Life with a Wife

I was able to perpetuate the conceit of the quintessential family man—beautiful estate home, beautiful children, days filled with creatively fulfilling work—all while indulging my childlike desire to be needed. Some call it a single life with a wife. Whatever the label, I was free to roam Los Angeles and other locales as a bachelor playboy when it suited me, and retreat into the swaddling of my home when I felt the need for that security. Maybe that's why the term is "playboy" and not "playman:" I was a man-child, masquerading as a responsible adult but acting every bit the unfaithful boy.

Unfaithful is a multi-dimensional word. Unfaithful to whom? Surely to Dana. But also to myself. To my children. *Un-faith-full.* One can't live on empty, devoid of faith, forever. Eventually, a vortex will engulf you, a helix of contradictions unravelling into a jumbled mess, simultaneously tangling all the competing narratives. The structure is too unstable: the building and decaying, the winding and unwinding— it cannot be sustained and will eventually crash to the ground.

Even in the face of my behavior, my resentment toward Dana thickened. As a confrontationist, my protestations and disappointments grew in frequency and intensity as time went on. I mistook my confrontations for honest attempts at addressing our problems. Rather than getting closer to any solution, however, my finger-pointing only focused attention on my frustration and anger. And besides, hadn't we made a pact *not* to discuss our emotional stew? Had I not been taking full advantage of my side of the bargain? Wasn't I now refusing to pay my consideration by forcing Dana to dig in the dirt with me? By pushing, I not only breached the emotional contract we had made, but I was also forcing her to burrow deeper.

Ah, the comforts of pathological compromise. For years, Dana and I managed the nuts and bolts of parenthood "for the kids" like a well-oiled machine. We rode out a marriage made in dystopian heaven, circling the drain, drifting apart and barely holding on.

As the man-made craft comprising my professional life flew closer to the sun, increasing amounts of unexamined childhood debris began to shake loose. Eventually, I could sense the unavoidable final break looming; the inevitable appointment with myself demanding a place on the calendar. In 2013, I gingerly stepped into the abyss and started meeting with Dr. Wood in an effort to find a more grounded existence. I pleaded with Dana to join me in therapy, but she was having none of it.

Faux Business

"Unexpressed expectations are premeditated resentments."

The bedrock of a marriage, or any relationship, is trust. Trust—as precious as it is fragile, a basic biological necessity that can only be built slowly and with consistency over time. We cannot act effectively without the comfort of being able to trust how others will respond. When trust breaks down in a relationship, our partner can suddenly and shockingly become our adversary, and fear grips the nervous system and takes control of the mind. Petty disagreements grow into violent communication, the fight or flight mechanism kicks into gear, and reason buries its head in the sand.

Trust was a rapidly-depreciating commodity in the twilight of my life with Dana. My world was on the verge of collapse by that time, and I was beginning to act out in all sorts of ways that were killing the trust in our marriage. My childhood experiences and man-child behavior had caught up with me. Time does not heal all wounds, as advertised. In my case, the pain from my childhood festered and metastasized into a debilitating emotional cancer that hurt the ones I needed the most, which is to say that I lacked trust in myself, and in the process, sabotaged any trust others had in me. And so, I began to dig into what I had done to erode trust, and why. I performed an emotional autopsy of a hijacked childhood that had led me to believe that, deep down, nothing mattered.

By the summer of 2014, the loan sharks were at the door, demanding the principal and accrued interest on the emotional credit I had borrowed. I was in London directing a Sky TV drama special I had written for Kiefer Sutherland and Stephen Fry called *Marked*. After completing principal photography, I received an offer for a multi-episode arc on the reboot of *Hawaii Five-0*. I promptly flew halfway around the world to the islands and filmed my first two episodes, then returned to London to finish the film and attend the premier, after which I flew back to Los Angeles to spend three days with my family before flying out to Hawaii again to continue filming before Dana and the boys joined me there on vacation. It would be the last family vacation we would ever have.

My life was, in other words, a maze of contradictions and superficial conceits. I was traveling the globe at the height of my professional success, but my world at home was falling apart. And my commitment to therapy, despite its virtues for me, only accelerated the explosive conclusion of my marriage.

That dynamic—therapy ushering the final act of divorce, rather than a rekindling of the marriage—is not uncommon. After the introduction of therapy into a long-suffering couple's silent war, this terrible trajectory is all too familiar: it's as if the two of you existed under intense pressure 20,000 leagues under the sea, and then were brought to the surface too quickly—everything implodes in the open air above the waves, and you suffer decompression sickness, the agony of the bends becoming too much to endure.

When locked in a trap of pathology packed as tightly as ours, new ideas are like fresh oxygen blowing on dying embers, whipping up a renewed conflagration that finally burns things to the ground. If one side of a couple is ready to confront demons while the other is not, the prospect of healing threatens the status quo and the unwilling partner resists, sometimes ferociously. What might fresh realizations do to the delicate psychological détente keeping things balanced in the dark? What would spill out of Pandora's Box?

The Affliction of Attorney Addiction

While a therapist demands we open up, a divorce lawyer seduces us with the promise to shut things down. How beguiling is the prospect of gaining the power to harness the legal and mental health systems and mold them into a weapon against the quiet desperation, frustration, and anger built up over decades? How intoxicating is the emotional tonic of bending these institutions to one's will, all in the single-minded service of publicly branding their now-loathed spouse as a fire-breathing dragon and banishing them forever—all while simultaneously maintaining the privacy of your own churning soul, sheltered from having to unpack your own burdens? Dana's choice got her what she wanted, but left carnage in its wake for me and our boys.

Ironically, when Dana built me into a heretic and burned me at the stake, she actually hastened my journey toward absolution while condemning herself to a continued emotional purgatory that, from my perspective, she may never escape. It took me years to realize this sole resolution from an otherwise hellacious experience. Being driven through the gauntlet of the divorce legal system makes emotional clarity exceedingly difficult to come by. Family courts, riven as they are with corruption and bias, frustrate a sense of personal responsibility and stoke one's instinct to hole-up in victimhood. Every step of the journey has left me feeling beat up and unfairly maligned, and I have wasted countless hours raging at the injustice, licking my wounds, indulging in grievance, and distracting myself from the hard work of accountability.

Even so, over the past six years, I have made progress in untangling Dana's conduct from my own, separating her outsized assault on my life from my own potent and reckless contributions to the downfall of our marriage. I have also managed to keep all of that separate from the decrepit clockworks of family law. But taking full responsibility for my words and deeds is another level. I often gain ground only to lose it again and claw back anew. It is difficult to know if one is succeeding in one's refusals of the lessons of family court's dystopian school of victimhood after spending so much time bloodied in its jaws.

Yet perhaps it is my turn, and respond, I will. With these words, I am standing up to my social murderer so that the body might receive a proper burial. It is difficult to know if I am responding with peak grace and bulletproof integrity—surely, such perfection is impossible to achieve. But that does not absolve me or anyone else from the responsibility of aiming for it.

CHAPTER 16

BACK FROM THE EMOTIONAL RUBICON

"Authenticity is the role of a lifetime."

"A mood disorder with mixed emotions."

Despite all I endured over the years—the pretense and insolence directed my way, the state-ordered prodding by psychiatrists and psychologists, all the bloody handcuffs unjustly inhibiting my movement, the systemic shackles restricting my behavior, the vultures of family law ripping into my psychological carcass—I never received an official mental health diagnosis any more unnerving than "a mood disorder with mixed emotions."

The diagnosis was a fair judgment if one must judge, a reasonable prognosis given the circumstances. I do not know one mother alive who wouldn't live with "mixed emotions" if she had been forcibly separated from her own flesh and blood for years. Should this sort of vague pronouncement on my internal state come anywhere close to being a valid justification to rip children from their loving, capable father? Don't most of us live with mixed emotions bubbling on the back burner, whether trapped in a divorce war that has pulled us from our children or not?

My mixed emotions, if that adequately describes the situation, were not simply the product of being forcibly separated from Charlie and Smith, but also a reaction to how that parental larceny transpired. This was parental dissociation conceived in malice, and effectuated in deceit. Both boys, I later discovered but did not know at the time, were interrogated by the DCFS in March 2015. They were ten and eight years of age at the time.

The imposition of that interrogation, and its purpose, obliterated the adolescent sense of safety and physical security they enjoyed with their father, one they had known since their birth. The overzealous investigator from the DCFS seemed motivated by a determination to destroy me rather than protect my children. This was, I hasten to add, the same lady (I learned months later) who had threatened Dana with taking our boys and placing them into foster care if she did not immediately procure a restraining order and file for divorce.

Reviewing the resulting DCFS report months later showed it to be a chilling monument to an unchecked department that appeared to have strayed dangerously from its core mission—that is, to protect children in need of protection. I was dumbstruck, among many other things, by the lingering innuendo expressed in the intrusive lines of questioning. I'm proud of my boys' resistance to the pressure foisted on them. They did not buckle under the appallingly leading questioning and appease the "official stranger" who had zero qualifications to conduct a psychological evaluation of my sons. Charlie and Smith knew they were safe in my presence, and both of them—despite the investigator's brazen attempt to put words in their respective mouths—told her so, in separate interviews and in no uncertain terms. That a department with a mandate to protect and serve children and families would wantonly violate the sanctuary of my boys' emotional and physical home in such an egregious manner is unforgivable. Nobody at the DCFS has been held accountable for the mayhem to which they subjected my family. The cartel of family law is indifferent to the destruction it causes to parents and children, and the catastrophic psychological scars it leaves in its wake.

The DCFS's obsessive focus on dismantling my relationship with Charlie and Smith was only one of the many battlements I was forced to defend. Dana and her counsel had by then embarked on a relentless campaign to have me declared psychologically damaged and thus dangerous. They did so through an unremitting stream of declarations and protestations—in the form of hundreds of court documents and dozens of hearings—that I was "bipolar" or "psychotic," or any other number of diagnostic criteria.

It was a shrewd, if unseemly and deceptive, tactic. It painted me as clinically insane to the judge, and they never deviated from that messaging. That not one medical practitioner, psychologist, psychiatrist, or independent evaluator, court-ordered or otherwise, had diagnosed any major mental illness, then or since, was an utterly immaterial fact to them. They weren't interested in the truth; they were invested in continuing to spin their narrative of "crazy dad." And those tactics worked in the Wild West that is family law, which, at least in my case, left me with no mechanism to challenge this synthetic construct and hold Dana or her lawyer accountable for their persistently false and baseless characterization of me.

That maddening lack of vetting or systemic rigor continued even after I momentarily waived my psychological medical privilege and agreed to an independent psychological evaluation by a court-certified psychiatrist in December of 2015. That psychiatrist issued a report unequivocally concluding that I had no mental illness. But those inconvenient facts were discarded by Dana and her lawyer, who contested the report in open court.

That independent three-day psychiatric evaluation and unilateral personality evaluation cost me in excess of $10,000. The psychiatrist checked monitor reports to see if there was any aberrant behavior reported. He obtained consultations on drug tests. He reviewed documents to see if, indeed, I had been dropped by an agent because of Dana's efforts. He also checked allegations that Smith had expressed suicidal ideation as well as my allegation that Dana was not cooperative and essentially disparaging me, and that the children had reported this. He looked into the monitor's reports (the monitor Dana selected) to determine if this was a reasonable belief or whether I was delusional. He also evaluated me by means of widely used personality tests.

All of which is to make clear this was an extensive evaluation. And the final report not only provided them with proof that their continued misdiagnoses of my psychological state of mind was utter fabrication, it also contained a summary and conclusions that were extremely damaging to Dana's credibility.

The reported findings are in fact an indictment of Dana's intellectual distortions and of the failure of the system to protect me against those distortions. The report observed, from several points of view—the psychiatrist's impressions, results of objective personality tests, the reports of professional therapists, monitor reports, and the impressions of colleagues—that I was "a steady, consistent, well-tempered individual" who could "modulate his responses to irritation as well as or better than the average custody litigant can." It went on to say that "the children are comfortable and trusting with their father according to the monitor reports" and, in contrast, "the children have reported to their father instances in which they have felt unsafe in their mother's home" and "it appears that mother has not facilitated the boys' relationship to father by helping them to feel confident in their relationship to their father. These statements were reported by the monitor." Perhaps the most disturbing finding was "The children did talk about mother having said something about killing their father."

The psychiatrist's summary of over sixty-nine monitor reports from April 21 to November 22, 2015, is damning in context, and ratified the extent of the parental alienation and malicious-mother syndrome my sons were experiencing during that initial period of separation from me and the extent to which they were afraid of their mother and wanted to be with their father. The evaluation also provided me with a clean bill of mental and moral health: "Mr. Ellis's allegations have an understandable basis, and are not the machinations of an illogical person."

The conclusions were indisputable and categorical but, alas, meaningless in the vortex of the family courts. Judge Iwasaki dismissed them when my lawyers presented in court, stating that he wasn't remotely interested in looking at the report. My frustration and sense of Orwellian seriality overtook me as my shock settled in and I realized this judge was unwilling even to read the evaluation. I boiled over in open court and blurted out, "What?! How can you . . . ?! This report disproves their entire narrative of me being insane." A swift ankle tap from my attorney and a stern look from the judge shut me up instantly. I knew the importance of presenting a calm demeanor—an ordered mood and unmixed emotions—in court, but even the well of the toughest of male giants can run dry when dealing with a "kick-the-can" judge in family law.

That judicially imposed lost opportunity was costly. It would be four torturous years before I was afforded another chance to endure the terror of psychological testing at the hands of a court-appointed medical expert and present for another psychological evaluation. But no matter. The findings were similar. A different judge (Iwasaki had been promoted) discarded the report in much the same way Judge Iwasaki expressed his indifference to any counter-narrative affirming my sanity.

• • •

The drumbeat of psychological trauma continued. In 2018 Dana and her counsel insisted on a child-custody evaluation, something I had vehemently opposed throughout the five-year proceedings because I did not want our boys to be forced to attend the courthouse. Ever.

But ever powerless, and with virtually no voice in court, the evaluation was approved. The morning designated for the evaluation,

I walked into the courthouse and suddenly heard Judy Bogen's voice shrieking, "It's him! Boys, turn around. Don't look at him! Bailiffs, BAILIFFS! Remove that dangerous man!! He has a restraining order!!!"

I turned around, and immediately laid eyes on Bogen, Dana, her mother, and my boys. Charlie and Smith appeared understandably confused and scared. They were thirty yards away, in the courthouse corridor, and I was merely walking to the designated courtroom. Bogen was manhandling the boys and forcibly turning them away from me, as if to convey that I posed some kind of threat to them. She then started remonstrating with court officials as she dramatically wagged her finger at me, her histrionics on full display. Dana and her mother just stared straight through me, cool, calm, collected, and determined in their obvious vengeance.

I turned and walked away to diffuse the situation. Standing in line at the coffee shop outside the courthouse moments later, I overheard two women cheerily discussing a family law case like a soap opera.

"I'm surprised the father hasn't killed himself." "I know, right?" "And do you know who the attorney for the mother is?" "It's not!" "It IS!" "Judy Bogen?!" "No wonder the father's paranoid. He doesn't stand a chance." "And their original social worker is now working in our department!" "Get OUT!" "It's t-RUE! I hear the DCFS case has been sealed so he'll never be able to access it." "Who's the evaluation with?" "Diana!!" The ladies howled with excitement. I was again crestfallen, a voyeur to talk of my own destruction.

I noted the lanyards hanging round their necks. These two ladies ran the custody-evaluation department. I couldn't resist and politely interjected with a smile, "You ladies seem to be enjoying yourselves."

Nonplussed by my introduction, they continued their very public overshare with a somewhat smug countenance. "Oh, we were just talking about this father who has no idea what he's up against."

I smiled. "Well, you know what I like to say," I responded. "Everything. Eventually. Connects." They paused, turned to each other, then nodded their appreciation. "Oh, I LIKE that!" "Yeah, that's GOOD!" A small moment of insolence and irony.

When I returned to the courthouse a few minutes later, I saw Dana inside the child-custody evaluation waiting room, intimately discussing my case with the social worker from the DCFS who'd interrogated my boys back in 2015. This social worker, who had left her position with the DCFS, was now working as a family court services specialist in the very department that would evaluate if and how much time I might legally be allowed to spend with my sons. Her colleague, Diana Devilliers, was our designated child-custody evaluator, and her superiors were the two ladies in line at the coffee shop moments earlier. The odds piled up against me.

The coffee-shop ladies returned to the custody evaluation room and went back to work behind the check-in counter without noticing me. Why would they? The "husband" to which they were referring during their storytelling was not a person, just an object that served as a punchline for their joke. But when they called my name and I appeared before them, you can imagine the look of horror on their faces when they realized that I was the dad they had been discussing with such odious and naked glee.

When called in for my interview, I was informed that Bogen was in a courtroom attempting to stall the evaluation and Ms. Devilliers could not begin until she received a directive that she could proceed from the judge. What followed was a ridiculous cat-and-mouse game as my attorney and I attempted to find out which courtroom Bogen was appearing in and whether we could even start the evaluation. Bogen's stall tactics predictably worked, and the evaluation was postponed. What followed was more hearings, more legal maneuvering, more posturing, more insinuations that I was clinically insane, and more attorney's fees and costs racked up by Bogen for her law firm.

When we eventually reconvened for the evaluation days later, I presented the entirety of my medical records to the evaluator so she could make a fully informed determination about my mental health. Yet Bogen again frustrated and stalled proceedings, and we eventually ended up in front of Judge Steven Cochran. Bogen, never tempered by intellectual integrity, launched into an argument that it was I who had stalled the child custody evaluation, and by 4:10 p.m. the judge had heard enough and closed the courtroom for the day because he had an important Dodgers playoff game to attend. The system has its priorities.

Another shock then ensued, and this one genuinely surprised. Soon after this hearing, Judy Bogen petitioned the court to be removed as counsel for Dana. Her new attorney informed me that Bogen had billed Dana well in excess of $1 million, was suing her for another $450,000 in unpaid fees, and that Bogen had never presented Dana with any of the settlement offers my attorney had made to end the case.

Although her former partners at Hersh Mannis Family Law removed her from the firm that used to bare her name, Judy Bogen still practices family law from a rented office in Sherman Oaks, a far cry from her salubrious high-rise in Beverly Hills. Dana now had to contend with the wrath of a woman who weaponizes her legal credentials to eviscerate families.

With Bogen exited, and having been served with an order to show cause and affidavit for contempt (over 100 counts), and with the threat of facing a criminal trial—different from the quasi kangaroo court of family law—Dana finally agreed to mediate. But after only two days, and with fees in excess of $31,000, she summarily cancelled mediation and dragged me back into court with her new attorney in tow, demanding that I subject myself to yet another psychological evaluation. And so, nearly four years after the first independent court-ordered psychological evaluation had proved my sanity and reported the litany of Dana's parental alienation maneuvers on our children, I reluctantly agreed to prove again what she and the court already knew—that I was not mentally unstable.

The details of the evaluation were Dana's prerogative, and from a list of available court-registered psychological evaluators, she selected adult, child, and adolescent forensic psychiatrist Suzanne M. Dupée to conduct my psychiatric evaluation. The cost for re-proving my sanity? Another $7,500. And yet again, four years later, the report's findings and conclusions were a virtual carbon copy of the first: "Greg is an enlightened, psychologically aware man who has been through a lot and has embraced intense psychotherapeutic work that has led him to be able to handle protracted high-conflict litigation and a barrage of negative and damaging descriptions towards him. I found no evidence that he presents a danger to the children in any way. In fact, the conjoint therapist reported that the boys do not feel their father is dangerous as their mother does. Further delays in reunification or stalling the legal process should be viewed as containing the estrangement between father and sons. Despite all the losses he has experienced, Greg remains emotionally strong and abnormally resilient." The report found "no evidence of abnormal or aberrant behavior by Greg reported by the monitors over the years" and "no mental illness."

When Judge Cochran was presented with the psychological evaluation, Dana's new counsel objected on the grounds that the report was "hearsay" until the court actually heard from the psychological evaluator in person. Her fee for court testimony was $4,500 per day (including being on call and travel time, as well as preparation time). It's no wonder the American Divorce Machine is such a cash-cow industry, raking in more than $60 billion a year at the expense of parents and children. And that's just the financial cost. The negative emotional impact on the individual and collective psychological well-being of families is incalculable. The cartel of family law is fueling a national mental health emergency that nobody is talking about. The personality of our United (mental) States of America is disturbed, disordered, and dysfunctional.

A Work in Progress

"A mood disorder with mixed emotions." Such are the delights of the DSM-5, the bible of psychiatric conditions and diagnostic criteria, a book woven together by professionals and ratified by their clubs. These days, outside the courtroom, our world is drowning in exhibitionistic blogging, vlogging, and flogging of DSM-5-verified subprime psychology. Social media is a broken spigot of opportunists promoting their embattled psyches; a cloudburst of performative sharing of defects and frailties; an infinite video wall of people revealing their scars. One would be hard-pressed to argue against the notion that collectively we just might be testing the limits of odious oversharing and naked narcissism.

I point this out in understanding of the tasty irony that—with this book and the accompanying video series and podcast—I am sharing my story in multimedia and so there is a contradiction to reconcile. While I believe we must decommission victimhood as a national currency and pump the brakes on pathological social media oversharing, at the same time I wonder at the alternative. After all, what are we to do—go back to the days when all the pain and anger backed up in a bottomless reservoir behind a dam of the damned? Where would all this anger be if not burning up Twitter? Is social media channeling anger into little controlled burns, or stoking things to an out-of-control conflagration?

For my part, I remain, without question, a work in progress. The steps I took that morning in March 2015, walking into Department 60 of the Los Angeles Superior Court, were profoundly fateful ones. I crossed over an invisible but solid border, leaving the United States of America to enter the dominion of family law—and that is a foreign land, one which quickly consumed and then discarded me without a whiff of the due process and other protections I thought I had as an American citizen. My resulting sense of isolation cannot be reduced to words. The world had turned on me and the speed of the pivot was so shocking, the sense of injustice so complete, it felt like being squeezed out of existence. And so, my journey of genuine self-discovery began, out of the ashes of an existence that had, in every objective sense, been incinerated. The lessons which had accumulated during my extended emotional vacation slowly revealed themselves and I, for the first time, was ready to receive them. That developing recognition has helped me cope with the aftermath of everything that has happened.

As I sifted through the debris of my life, salvaging what was worthy, I began to catch glimpses of a new reality. The moments where I wasn't so alone have, for example, increased steadily over time and have lessened the harshness of the lessons, which allowed me to better synthesize some of the shame. That awful feeling—that I was the author of my own demise—continues to be assuaged as I work to unearth the mass grave of fathers who walked into a family courtroom completely foreign from the America they had been so convinced lay just outside the doors.

And thus, a new nerve in my restless psyche was aroused. I believe that by talking and sharing I might help others rise up and find their path to a better place, and it is that spirit that animates these pages. Others who understand that, at the heart of this culture so steeped in the exposition of our internal turmoil, there exists a system of indulgences within family law where the rights enjoyed by the masses don't apply to mere mortal men; a system that refuses to receive the shortcomings and vulnerability of empathetic, honest men.

Emotions are Feelings with Memories Attached

There remains the issue of anger, and it can be a slog up a muddy hill at times. The frustration over my family disintegration and the subsequent spiriting away of my boys has been among the most difficult emotional challenges to contend with. I reasoned, I reconciled, I preached, and I attempted to govern myself through understanding. I embraced various therapies and all forms of emotional sobriety—and yet I was so angry over what Dana had done that, in the darkness of my many restless nights, I surrendered to my rage. The work is never done, and the damages are never paid.

Anger is the forbidden fruit of emotions. All spiritual traditions and pathways explore the human relationship to anger. For example, wrath is one of Christianity's seven deadly sins, and anger and hatred are one of the Three Poisons of the Tibetan Buddhist "Wheel of Life."

Ironically, in the era of Trump, media companies—from CNN to Fox News to Twitter—peddled anger for cash. But in our face-to-face lives, any display of anger must be stamped out immediately, lest a swear word be misconstrued as a declaration of war.

I believe this is a false and dangerous paradigm, because our animus, our rage—*our outrage*—is often a natural barometer signaling important information about ourselves. Not aggressive or violent outbursts of anger—dirty anger—which must be quelled and channeled, but rather natural, healthy, responses to direct attacks or provocations—clean anger. The latter is often the canary in the coal mine, announcing humiliation, heartache, anxiety, depression, disappointment, fear.

Epistemologist Dr. Gary David says, "Anger involves sensations felt as 'way too much.' Thought grabs the feeling and connects it to a scene. Backed up anger is a life of denial of the feeling. For example, feeling shame because you're feeling angry: 'I shouldn't feel that.'"

Dr. Ryan Martin, chair of the Psychology Department at the University of Wisconsin-Green Bay, explains the value of healthy, or "clean" anger: "Anger is a motivator. Just as your thirst motivates you to get a drink of water, the same way your hunger motivates you to get a bite to eat, your anger can motivate you to respond to injustice."

I am living proof. Dana had legitimate reasons to be angry at the injustices I foisted on her in our marriage, and I had legitimate reasons to be angry at the injustices Dana imposed on me. But when we walked into the offices of Divorce Corp., one of us was cheered on, urged to fashion anger into a weapon with unlimited firepower and without concern for proportion, while the other was prohibited from even the slightest display of emotion even under constant attack. That is injustice in its purest form.

Inner Dialogue is the Poem of Anxiety

I acknowledge wholeheartedly that there were times in my marriage when I expressed my irritations poorly. Now, when anger arrives, I have learned to hear what it has to say; to pay attention to what my body is trying to tell me; to tune in and listen to the inner voice explaining my wounds and confusion over the rushing of blood in my ears. I've learned to talk myself back into a mature state of mind.

My recovery continues, and I labor to place Dana's actions in context, as I do my own. I endeavor to feel my anger rather than suppress it—to understand it, accept it, and, in the process, harness and contain it.

Confusing Love with Desire

I have come to believe that fundamental to our greatest flourishing is a deeper understanding of love that runs counter to our instinct and socialization. In her book *Cruel Optimism*, author and Professor of English at the University of Chicago, Lauren Berlant, pins modern life to a backdrop of affect theory, and illuminates how often something we desire is actually an obstacle to our greater needs. "All attachment is optimistic," Berlant says, "because it is an attempt to grasp for something beyond ourselves and enter into the world in order to bring closer the satisfying something that you cannot generate on your own but sense in the wake of a person, a way of life, an object, project, concept, or scene."

It is not our fault: love drives us toward attachment, and this yearning to connect is at the core of being human. One need not be a student of affect theory or a disciple of Jung to understand this universal treasure of wisdom about human nature—it can be found by many paths.

The Buddha said it as clearly as one can: "The root of suffering is attachment." Buddhism teaches that life's natural state of being is change, and by desiring someone or something, one is essentially trying to control and make permanent something that is naturally impermanent.

Our relationship between love and attachment must be confronted, and the quality of love must be understood in the context of the pain and bewilderment that comes with inevitable detachment. The seeming inconsistency between loving someone and then moving beyond this understanding to something more compassionate and separate from need is a huge project to tackle. For some, wrangling with this seeming paradox between loving and leaving—between closeness and separation, and between celebrating and grieving—is more difficult than for others.

Becoming Less Emotionally Dependent

Connecting the dots of my life has meant unpacking familial baggage and understanding that the emotional neglect I experienced in my youth made me much more susceptible to a dysfunctional understanding of love. My childhood was a constant grasping for parental love inevitably withheld.

I was seven years old when my mother informed me that I had forgotten her birthday. I rushed away, consumed with shame, and begged, stole, and borrowed enough money to buy her a box of chocolates. Upon presentation, she sneered with contempt and said, "It's a bit late now, isn't it?"

During my first year of high school, I won the coveted Sportsman of the Year award. I competed in four events—javelin, high jump, 200, and 800 meters—and came in first all around. I returned home in jubilant mood with my coveted prize, prouder than I had ever felt in my life, positive that my parents would surely notice me now—they had to! But my success didn't even register when I told my mum. She was too concerned with overcooking the evening's fish finger and chips dinner and presenting it as *haut de cuisine* to notice me, let alone my trophy. My father didn't bat an eyelid when I tried to tell him. This pattern would repeat itself throughout my childhood.

I recall vividly the morning I left home at the age of seventeen, my mother yelling at me from the kitchen about something inconsequential. As I walked away, severing the umbilical cord of shame and anger that consumed the only world I had ever known, every step I took from my mother's door brought a corresponding and palpable sense of relief. Whatever trauma and heartbreak might have awaited me, whatever glory or success, whatever life would shove down my throat, I would swallow it all to escape this original dysfunction.

Along my journey, devoid of self-worth and deprived of real value by my parents, I responded instinctively and went thrill-seeking, searching for value outside myself. With relationships, I climbed aboard the relational rollercoaster ride at an early age, becoming a love addict, always searching for the next high sparked by a new connection. Partners came and went until eventually I found myself drowning in a cocktail of intoxicating heartbreak. I forever teetered at the altar of potential romantic dividends that could never be harvested, reeling in a tangled web of shame and self-loathing.

I have since come to understand that a middle child like me within a family dynamic like mine often takes on (or is pushed into) a hero role, losing integrity in exchange for a more adult role, often becoming "the expert" overachiever who keeps it all together, trying to mask the family's failures. Oftentimes, these "hero" children wake up much later in life to a nice home, a fancy car, a high-paying job, and a supposedly perfect family, only to find they want to trade it for something more authentic. This emotional current tugged at me throughout my life, but I became fully conscious of the rocky shoals of self-destruction and aware of my thirst for authenticity only after I had been stripped of everything I had worked for.

In *The Eden Project,* James Hollis explores this common confusion about love; this yearning for dependency or attachment that we all share as we move through life, tailed closely by our childhood pain and losses. His words resonate in my conscience: "We struggle to . . . give up our deepest longing for homecoming—its challenge to grow up, take responsibility, to be an adult instead of a child. We always carry that frightened child within, and the power of the adult we seek to become must be balanced against the demands of the child." The tired child inside each of us is furious at how long they have been neglected and in pieces. If we are born in pain, we are reborn in unity. The poet Rumi echoes the same sentiment in haunting and deeply personal terms: "We feel the longing so deeply because we have tasted the union."

Longing becomes more poignant if we cannot tell if a friend is going away or coming back. And so, it is in that spirit that I emerge from the battleground of family law, bloody but unbowed, pushing ahead, determined to honor the precious child within me and exercise fidelity to the adult I have become.

To those I may have wronged

Please forgive me.

To those I helped,

I wish I had done more.

To those I neglected to help,

I ask for understanding.

To those who helped me,

I can never thank you enough.

This is the denouement of my divorce.

CHAPTER 17

FATHERHOOD
AND FUNERALS

"Everything. Eventually. Connects."

"Everything you're trying to reach—by taking the long way round—
you could have right now, this moment. If you'd only stop thwarting
your own attempts. If you'd only let go of the past, entrust the future
to Providence, and guide the present toward reverence and justice.

Reverence: so you'll accept what you're allotted, Nature intended
it for you, and you for it.

Justice: so that you'll speak the truth, frankly and without
evasions, and act as you should—and as other people deserve."

These are the sage words of Marcus Aurelius from *Meditations*,
written two thousand years ago. His stoic teachings might be a little
out of step with the fashions of our day, but for my money there may
be no better guide to manhood.

Alas, the final act of this drama must be faced. I am a father,
but my boys have been taken from me. How can I respond to that
devastating fact and live the life I want and need to live? I can navigate
that suffocating pain only one way—with integrity, both to my own

sense of responsibility and in my engagement with the world around me. As psychologist Dr. Jordan B. Peterson famously put it, before we strive to change the world, we first must clean up our own rooms and make our own beds. Because it is there where we must lie every night hoping for the respite of sleep, and it is from there that we must wake each morning with renewed vigor, vowing to do better, becoming more conscious of what got in the way to our doing better. Our lines of inquiry, the wounds we each must heal, these we must uncover alone, but the good news is that the information is not difficult to access. We know in our souls which behaviors make us feel weak and uncomfortable. The voice is always there, murmuring, and it does not take much silence, stillness, or honesty for the tentative whisper to build to a shout.

I believe in this form of conscientiousness, and at the same time acknowledge that parts of this book work to put my life in the context of outside forces and lay culpability at the feet of the legal system and of those who evade their own responsibilities by exploiting its escape clauses. These two realities are not incompatible—yes, the system is corrupt, and yes, Dana's disappointment and anger justified in her mind a disproportionate response that I did not deserve. And everything beyond that I must own, learn from, grow beyond, and respond to authentically.

I have discussed at length my sense that society is in a bit of a freefall, with fathers as the fall guys. This diminishment of the father has metastasized into an emotional exigency for our children, one which urgently demands attention. I hope I have gone some way in illuminating the systematic and pervasive marginalization of boyhood, manhood, and fatherhood and the branding of masculinity as toxic by definition, and have attempted to do so without encouraging more victimhood. I urge you to trust your own experience. If you feel your fatherhood is under attack, no matter how starkly that viewpoint stands in the face of the common wisdom you may have been fed in your travels, it is not your imagination.

If I can get to higher ground, so can you. But in the end, it is not about my life, or even the lives of fathers whose parenting rights have been destroyed by an unfeeling, corrupt system—it is about protecting our children and doing all we can to clear a path so that they might reach their full potential. With all the challenges facing children today, they need their fathers more than ever.

A Funeral for My Boys

I did not want to write this book—I *had* to. While this is a story about my tumultuous journey to uncover mysteries and reclaim innocence, I trust it will feel familiar to many walking a similar path. And so, I offer *The Respondent* with the hope that it helps just one man know himself and the world more honestly, and helps just one child avoid the loss of a loving parent.

I submit this to forsaken fathers not only as a totem that stands to remind you that you are not alone, but also as a map to help you in your disconsolate quest for enlightenment and redemption, as you exorcise the unrelenting demons of living grief that come with missed milestones, lost childhoods, stolen moments, broken promises, disillusioned unions, and all the skeletal remains of bygone days. This is my testimony to those cast out: you deserve to be back in the village. You belong.

The Respondent is also for those who love a man enduring a separation, for a father of a father, a mother, a brother, a sister, or a child. If you know someone going through a difficult divorce or the loss of their children, please reach out to them. If they don't grab your hand right away, try again—they may eventually accept it and love you for it. You just might save a life.

All of that said, *The Respondent* is a cautionary tale. After more than half a decade of trying to get back to my kids through the courts, desperately attempting to secure a co-parenting arrangement—allowing them to have their father present and me to participate meaningfully in my sons' lives—I have laid down my cross and surrendered this destructive battle. I've exhausted myself resisting the perpetual assault on my fatherhood, and every fiber of my being wants to maintain the resistance. But the road to wisdom is a long and tortuous one, and for me it ends with the realization that this fight is an exercise in futility, one that is exacting too high a price on the boys. And so, I have chosen to quit fighting in vain. I could not have imagined, when I began this book, reaching this point—I was still very much in the fight, and single-mindedly focused on reclaiming my fatherhood. And yet, after years of being flushed through the divorce court rinse cycle, I realized that the system won't allow it. Dana won't allow it. The world we live in won't allow it. The undeniable fact is that my role of father has been cut short, my character killed off by authors beyond my control. Dana succeeded in rendering me dead to my boys—aided and abetted by the cartel of family law. Together they conspired to steal my freedom, kidnap our children, and murder my family.

And so, even as I cheer you on, my fight for my own fatherhood stops here. This may seem like giving up or failing my boys, or relinquishing my role as their father, but I don't see it that way. I see sparing the boys the further torture of this process as the ultimate act of fatherhood. There is no way forward for me that doesn't involve forcing Smith and Charlie under the microscope—pinning them down on flypaper for further analysis, putting them in a position where they are torn between divergent allegiances and filled with the fear of saying the wrong thing or letting someone down—all under the scrutiny of clinical professionals who don't know or love them as I do. I will not do that to them. Never again. I am choosing instead to love them and set them free.

My boys have lost so much. I have lost so much. I will never be there when they come home from school with a big teenage victory to share or a hidden heartache. I will never see them off to high school prom with their first loves, or throw them the car keys with the trembling fear that comes with letting them spread their wings.

We will never get to play football in the park. We have been denied those rites of passage that define parenthood and childhood—I am forsaken; they are lost to me, and I to them.

For me, the pain of this ultimate cancellation has been immense. For them, it is surely much more complicated.

In an effort to wash the ache away, I had a small ceremony for this passing, a funeral to bury all the lost years and love that should have been ours to share. I will continue forward on my path, my arms always extended wide in invitation, filled with hope and faith that they find their way back to me when they have grown.

With this book, I officially shed the role of Respondent and take on the role of Petitioner—not a petitioner cloaked in victimhood, resentment, or fear, but one rising as a bold architect of a better future, building anew with love and commitment. *The Respondent* is *my* petition, both for the lost child in me finding his way home, and for my lost children, Charlie and Smith. The bond we forged shall never fully be torn asunder, not by Dana nor the system that enabled her destructive rage.

Charlie and Smith, my beautiful boys,

I love you both with all that I am, unconditionally and forever, and if you're reading then I meant to say men, because that's what you're becoming. I am, and will remain, extraordinarily proud of you, both of who you are and of the strength and courage you've displayed in overcoming a titanic trauma that no child should ever be forced to endure. Your strength infuses me with the will to go on, rendering me hopeful we will be together again, in better times. No one can stop that, not even the family law system with all its array of forces. I am resolved to be the Petitioner, and I will petition you with my love until my last breath is taken.

Love always,

Dad

EPILOGUE

"Surrender is giving up your version of the story."

"The unexamined life is not worth living," as Socrates intoned some 2,400 years ago. A pithy refrain for a giant of Greek philosophy, to be sure, but one worth considering as we chart our way through this short, harsh, and yet occasionally euphoric life we are given. Examination is what lies before me as I brace for the postscript of my now dissolved marriage and all it has wrought in my life.

The task is a tall one, because my emotional and spiritual energy has for the last six years been devoted to this book and its chronicling of my harrowing experience. Every twitch and torque I committed to paper, every revelation I followed with a note and notion of where it might find its way into my story, and all my psychological anxiety I channeled into the service of this literary catharsis. Now it is complete. My story is told. And yet, my life remains. The debris is scattered everywhere, and the void awaits as I pick up the pieces.

Those pieces serve as a veritable minefield challenging my gait and occasionally slowing my pace. I was forty-six years old when the police rapped on my door in March 2015, but I nonetheless felt young. I was in good physical—if not emotional—health, and I persisted in living the life of a young man. I traveled the world, briskly walked the mahogany-lined halls of my country club, and trafficked in expensive restaurants and Hollywood hangouts. But divorce robbed that youth, depriving me of five years consumed instead with anxiety and basic survival and subjecting me to a mountainous heap of vitriolic smelt. Now, on the other side of it, I feel emotionally aged, but not old. And so, I fight the sensation that I have forged a curious anticlimax—I have invested so much in telling this tale of my life-defining experience, and yet so much of that life is still unlived, awaiting examination. My age does not allow a graceful stroll into the final sunset, because I find myself in the lateness of a harsh and stormy summer, with autumn beckoning. And so, I must author a sequel, not one narrating a past trauma, but rather that of a life well lived with the time the universe allows me.

I intend to spend that time wisely, deploying the lessons I learned from the five-year odyssey of my divorce from Dana. So much has changed, and I am so different now, but I take one resolution with me as I chart the path forward—not merely to make new mistakes and not repeat the old ones, but to receive the most telling and uplifting lesson I learned in losing everything: the world promises friendship when you're riding high, but your real friends will reveal themselves when the pretext of money and success are stripped away. I learned that punishing lesson the hard way. Countless Hollywood types who had promised lifelong friendship scattered as I was defamed and defeated in court. But others emerged, and often under the most unexpected circumstances. The morning of the first day of my DVRO trial, I was standing in a coffee shop outside the Stanley Mosk Courthouse, waiting in line behind a tall lawyer. We struck up a conversation, one that prior to March 5, 2015, would undoubtedly have consisted of a spate of pleasantries followed by parting ways, never to cross paths again—but this particular morning, already a changed man betrayed by many, I actually spoke to this lawyer, Todd

Lander, and we agreed to have lunch. To my surprise we have since become close friends—Todd has supported me, assisted with this book, and proven to be the type of "foxhole" friend others vowed to be but were not.

There are others who likewise punctuated my life as I walked over the coals of what was left after Dana finished with me. Indeed, despite possessing only a fraction of the material wealth I did before March 5, I am a much richer man; I am healthier, emotionally sober, ready to keep my side of the street clean, and surrounded by friends who are real—not imagined—supporters.

The Hollywood dream has dissipated, and thank God for that.

The darkness is passed. The dawn beckons. The future is bright. I am ready.

FADE TO BLACK.

MEDICAL RECORDS

1st COURT-ORDERED PSYCHIATRIC EVALUATION
December 9, 2015

CARL F. HOPPE, PH.D.

Suite 215
360 North Bedford Drive
Beverly Hills, CA 90210
(310) 550-0314
FAX 276-4825

Unilateral Personality Evaluation

JRMO: ELLIS

LASC Case No. BD 617 933
Hearing Date December I 0, 2015
Before Hon. Diesman

CONFIDENTIAL—DO NOT DUPLICATE OR DISTRIBUTE

IRMO: ELLIS

Scope of this report: Greg Ellis eagerly presented himself for a personality evaluation. He said this was needed by the Court to determine if there was a continuing need for him to be monitored, as he had time with his two children, 11 year old Charlie and 9 year old Smith. Mr. Ellis stated after a court hearing on August 6, 2015, "The Judge said he needed to hear from an expert to get rid of monitored visitation . . ."

Limitations of this report: I have not seen the children in this matter. I therefore cannot recommend custodial arrangements except to the extent I can comment if Mr. Ellis has the profile of a parent who ordinarily would be monitored. . . . I did read the most recent Court Proceeding submitted to me, which was of May, 2015. I called 9 collateral witnesses. . . . I do have sufficient information to render an opinion as to Mr. Ellis's capacity for good judgement and impulse control based on multiple sources of information, such as personality tests, monitor reports, documents, my own clinical impressions, other mental health professionals' opinions, and other sources. These sources of information are both current and archival.

Procedures:
To evaluate Mr. Ellis, I used the following procedures:

- Observations and orientation to testing
- The Minnesota Multiphasic Personality Inventory (MMPI-2)
- The Millon Clinical Multiaxial Inventory (MCMI-III)
- The Rorschach Inkblot Method of Personality Assessment
- The Parent Awareness Skills Survey, spontaneous level only (PASS)

- Detailed History Questionnaire (DHQ)
- Review of documents: Monitored visits, Drug Test Results, Character References, Court Documents of May 1, 2015; various emails.
- Behavioral Observations
- Consultation with DMG Drug Testing Facility
- Collateral calls.

Interview Impressions: Mr. Ellis was prompt, arriving a few minutes early for each of two appointments. He was oriented as to where he was, logical in his statements, and alert as to time and dates. He was well groomed and adequately dressed. As we discussed his present custody arrangements, Mr. Ellis was logical and appropriate. His affect generally matched what he said. He had a sardonic sense of humor. He reacted with appropriate emotions to the content of what was being said by himself or by me.

Mr. Ellis is particularly concerned, because one drug test reflected residual opiates. He explained that he had eaten a lemon poppy seed muffin. A brief check on the internet reveals many references to the fact that oral consumption of poppy seeds will result in urinalysis with peak values of approximately 10.0 micrograms per liter. For example, the Journal of the Annals Toxicology 2003 January-February; 27 (1); 53-6 "Urinary Concentrations of Morphine and Codeine after Consumption of Poppy Seeds," Thevis M, Opfermann G, Schanzer. I have also consulted DMG Drug Testing Facility to interpret the drug screening of July 2015 in which opiates and Codeine were said to have been detected. The proprietor confirmed that poppy seeds can cause this level of opiate detection.

Mr. Ellis characterized the children as reporting that their mother has said negative things about him. He believes that he is being pushed into what he called an abyss of character assassination. Thus, without using the term, he, in effect, described his belief that the children's mother attempts to alienate the children from him. Monitor reports were checked to see if this is accurate. The monitor did quote the children as relaying several remarks they attributed to their mother that confused them about whether their father was a sick man or not. The children did talk about mother having said something about killing their father. . . .

Mr. Ellis's allegations have an understandable basis, and are not the machinations of an illogical person.

Mr. Ellis is also concerned that his son, Smith, has allegedly talked about wanting to end his life, that life is useless. Monitor reports were checked to see if this is accurate. I found quotations from the monitor to this effect.

Mr. Ellis spoke of his regret for having broken into his own house, when his wife attempted to lock him out. He broke a small pane of glass in order to get into a back door. He said he feels responsible for entering his home in this manner. The Department of Children & Family Services (DCFS) was called to the home for this and other occasions. He alleged that the investigations have been closed as unfounded. There was a time when DCFS had temporarily placed him on a list of child abusers. This, however, was reversed after he appealed.

Mr. Ellis also alleged that his estranged wife called his agent and persuaded the agent to terminate professional relations, by telling the agent that Mr. Ellis had many psychological problems and would be trouble. He believes because of his wife's undermining his efforts, "many deals went away." I checked with court documents to determine if this was a credible allegation or the result of some delusion. Court documents did indeed make reference to an agent dropping him due to his wife's calls.

Thus, Mr. Ellis raises several issues. To assess his rationality, I checked monitor reports to see if there was any aberrant behavior reported. I obtained consultation on drug tests. I reviewed documents to see if, indeed, he had been dropped by an agent because of his wife's efforts. I also checked allegations that Smith has expressed suicidal ideation by checking monitor reports. Mr. Ellis alleged mother was not cooperative and essentially disparaging him, and that the children reported this. I looked into the monitor's reports to determine if this was a reasonable belief or whether it was delusional. I also evaluated him by means of widely used personality tests.

Document Review:

Monitor Reports: The monitor's reports are voluminous, and I have prepared a summary of these, reducing them to 6 ½ pages. This summary is attached to the body of this report as appendix A and made by this reference a part of the report. The monitor reports are particularly valuable because they present more than six dozen behavioral observations made between April 21, 2015, and November 22 of 2015. Perhaps nothing predicts future behavior as well as past behavior, especially recent past behavior. There are times in adults' lives when substantial change of personality is more likely than at other times. One of these is the time of marriage. Another is the birth of a child. Death of a loved one and especially death of a parent can precipitate change. Filing divorce presents another window of possible change of behavior. These monitor reports reflect Mr. Ellis's behavior with the children since the onset of the divorce process. They are instructive for what the father has been observed to do with the boys as well as what he has been observed not to do with them.

What father did was to discipline them verbally. He was observed to be affectionate with the children, and the boys' affection for him was frequently, usually, and excitedly returned, according to the monitor. Father facilitated the boys' relationship with their mother by repeatedly telling them to listen to their mother. He taught the boys about fair play, about sharing, and about racial innuendos which the boys observed. He reassured the boys when they brought him concerns about the financial effects to them. . . . He behaved appropriately and temperately on every one of 69 occasions during the recent six months from April to October, 2015.

Here is what he did not do. Father did not use the children's statements about their mother to inflame or exploit their concerns to his advantage. He did not discuss details of the financial arrangements or questions about the events leading to divorce and the legal process, even if the boys asked about such things. He would reassure and distract or delay answering, telling them such things as they would learn more when they got older. He did not denigrate the boys' mother, even if they quoted her as telling them their father was sick or "bio-polar" (bipolar). He did not exploit the boys' knowledge, or the incident during which one of the boys was bitten on the face by a dog at home. He did not inflame the boys when they wished to have overnights with him or go away to Hawaii or Japan with him. In the monitor's reports of the boys' statements to their father we get a glimpse of Smith and Charlie's perception of their mother. They seem to blame her for not letting their father come home.

Drug Tests:
Recognizing that the analysis of drug tests is beyond my usual scope of practice, I contacted the DMG drug labs in West Los Angeles, which I regularly and frequently used to access custody litigants when there are allegations of drug abuse. On June 30 opiates were detected. Mr. Ellis claimed he had consumed some poppy seeds. My consultant said that a positive test less than 600ng with no history of opioid abuse indicates probable poppy seed ingestion. Mr. Ellis's test was 300ng.

The Court Transcript from May 1, 2015: I reviewed this transcript primarily to determine if father's allegations about purported vindictiveness of the boys' mother were based on evidence or based on delusion. There is a reference in the document to father's agent dropping father as a client because of a call from mother alleging that father would be a problem, advising agent not to send him out for work.

Discussion:
According to the most widely used personality inventory, he is well within normal limits on all important dimensions and in some respects better adjusted than the average custody litigant is. This is not to say he is perfect, but the question arises as to why he must be monitored while he is with his children.

More than five dozen monitor reports are exemplary. No critical incidents of his own making were noted. His children are seen to be positively attached to him and openly affectionate with him. He is responsive to this. The children are reported often to have quoted their mother making inflammatory or derogative comments about their father, which irritates them. In contrast, there are several instances of Mr. Rees turning such comments aside and facilitating mother's interaction with the children by reminding them to be respectful and attentive to her. He has refrained from discussing legal details of the marital dispute and Court procedures even when the children have become aware of these from some other source.

The results of computer-scored personality tests, my own impressions, the impressions of his therapist of two years, monitor reports, collateral and informants, and drug tests are consistent enough that I have considerable confidence in the conclusions of this report.

Summary and Conclusions:

From several points of view: my impressions; results of objective personality tests; the report of Mr. Ellis's professional therapist; monitor reports and the impressions of colleagues, Mr. Ellis is a steady, consistent, well-tempered individual.

On psychological testing he is well within the range experienced from other custody litigants. He perceives conditions allowing for multiple interpretations as many other individuals do. Test data suggest Mr. Ellis can modulate his responses to irritation as well as or better than the average custody litigant can. . . . Objective psychological tests are well within normal limits.

Extensive drug testing has been done. A few anomalies have been found in the drug tests. According to my consultant at the DMG drug lab, these anomalies can be accounted for by his explanation that he ate poppy seeds resulting in trace opiates in his urine sample.

The children are comfortable and trusting with their father, according to the monitor reports. I have prepared a summary of these many reports and attach them as Appendix A of this report.

In contrast the children have reported to their father instances in which they have felt unsafe in their mother's home due to a dog which actually attacked Smith and bit him on the face or due to threats to hit them which they attributed to their uncle Dres. According to the monitors reports, Mr. Ellis did not take advantage of these accidents and incidents to inflame the children against her mother. On the contrary he was observed to make comments facilitating the boys' respect and obedience to their mother. From the boys' comments about father being "bio-polar" or "doctors say he's sick," it would seem father would have had an opportunity to attempt to make the boys' relationship to their mother worse, but he did not do so.

In contrast, from the boys' statements to their father, it appears that mother has not facilitated the boys' relationship to father by helping them to feel confident in their relationship to their father. These statements were reported by the monitor. Court documents suggest mother has also interfered with father's relationship to professionals, such as his agent. From the point of view of these several kinds of observations, the need for continuing monitoring of Mr. Rees and his children is questionable. . . . I trust this has been an adequate response to your request for testing. If further information is needed, and/or questions remain, do not hesitate to call.

Respectfully submitted,

Carl F. Hoppe, PH.D.
(PSY 4070)
CFH:laf

APPENDICES

Appendix A

CARL F. HOPPE, PH.D.
SUMMARY OF 69 MONITOR REPORTS
April 21 to November 22, 2015

April 21   The children were happy and hugged and kissed their father, and said "I missed you." I noted father facilitated interaction with the grandpa, presumably maternal grandfather. *No CI (critical incident) reported.*

April 25   Smith embraces his father. He said he was confused because his mother told him his dad is sick. Smith continued, "Mom said that if you try to pull us in the car and take us away to not listen to you," and Mom said that he has "bio polar." *No CI.*

April 28   The boys said, "This is the best night out ever." *No CI.*

May 3   The children hugged and kissed father. Smith said, "Mom says you are still sick." Charlie said, "I wish it was Saturday because I want to spend more time with you." *No CI.*

May 5   The boys "hugged and kissed MP (Father)," according to the monitor. Smith told father "I'm confused that you say you are not sick, but Mom says that two doctors say that you are sick." Father

responded, "I know it's confusing, but I love you."
The boys asked to go on a trip to Japan or Hawaii
with their father. *No CI.*

May 7   The boys hugged and kissed their father. Everyone
appeared to have fun, according to the monitor.
No CI.

May 12   Again hugs and kisses upon greeting father. Charlie
asked, "Daddy, Mommy said you were going to
stay away for a year. Is that true? Are you going to
miss my birthday?" Father responded, "I hope not."
No CI.

May 15   Smith ran and jumped into his father's arms
upon meeting him. Smith worried, "I don't want
Mommy to use her money because we might lose
our house." *No CI.*

May 16   Saw dad's rented house, explored it. Smith spoke
about maybe having to change schools. Asked dad if
he owned shares of Apple, if he would sell them, and
if mom had an interest in them. Smith asked dad
to give some money to mom, adding, "I don't want
to change schools." Some sibling wrestling; Charlie
complained about it. *No CI.*

May 19   Again hugs and kisses for dad. Charlie said in
relevant part, "Mom . . . says that you (Dad) are
crazy." Father responded, "It's OK to express your
feelings." Charlie added, "I hate my life." He added,
"I'll be mad at her (Mom) if she doesn't let you
come back." Father responded, "It's a difficult time

for you and Mom and you don't need to be mad at Mom." Charlie continued by saying his mother told him two doctors say dad is bipolar. *No CI.*

May 21   The children said they asked their mom about dad coming back. "Mom said she's not letting you come home because you did something inappropriate to her." Dad responded in relevant part, "These are grown-up discussions." *No CI.*

May 23   The children were happy about seeing dad. Again there was talk about mom not letting dad come home. Dad facilitated obedience to mom: Are you listening to your mom?" Smith responded, "You (Dad) give me good discipline." Dad replied, "You need to listen to your mom." Smith again brought up financial concerns: "Dad, can you pay for school? . . . I don't want to switch schools." Charlie asked dad to promise to help his mommy with the payment for the house and school. Charlie said, "Mom says you are lying to us." *No CI.*

May 26   *No CI.*

May 28   Charlie hugged his father, saying, "I just want you to come home." Smith added, "Mom is really mad. She's not letting you come back. . . . She said . . . she does not know if we'll keep the house or school." Father asked if Smith was OK, and suggested they go back to his home. *No Cl.*

May 31   Smith said to his father, "I'm sad that you are gone." The children yelled to dad, "I love you" as the monitor took them home. *No CI.*

June 2	Charlie said, "I'm furious at Mom . . . because she loves you but won't let you come back. I'm going to talk to her about it." Smith complained among other things "life is being really hard." *No CI.*
June 4	The two boys greeted their father with hugs and kisses. *No CI.*
June 7	The two boys would occasionally come to their father, and they hugged him. Charlie complained "the house feels empty when you aren't there." Dad encouraged the children to listen their mother at home. *No CI.*
June 10	Charlie and Smith greeted their father with hugs and kisses. Charlie complained his mother was upset with him yesterday. Dad did not inflame this. Smith complained, "Uncle Dres is mean. . . . I was stretching and he said he was going to stretch his fist on my face." Smith said this made him feel scared. Charlie said he was afraid of Uncle Dres doing this to him too. Smith offered to stay with his father instead of being at home with Uncle Dres. *No CI.*
June 11	Again the children greet their father with hugs and kisses. Smith complained, "Mom doesn't believe me. I don't feel safe with Uncle Dres." Smith said, "Dres was going to punch me in the face." As they were leaving the father they called from the car, "I love you, Dad." *No CI.*
June 14	Again the children greet their father with hugs. Father managed a physical dispute between the

boys, asking them to apologize. Mother monitored jokes, telling them they were getting inappropriate. Charlie complained that people at school asked if their father is taking drugs. Smith stated that mother leaves him home alone as she takes the dog for a walk. Charlie said this did not happen. Father did not exploit this complaint. *No CI.*

June 16   Charlie said, crying, "I want to have sleepovers and maybe do one week with you and one week with Mom." He continued, "I want to have more time with you but we are not allowed." *No CI.*

June 18   Again the children greet their father with hugs and kisses and jokes. *No CI.*

June 21   Again hugs and kisses from the children. Father appropriately corrected the children about using inappropriate words and inappropriate jokes. A dispute arose about whether Smith would have dinner with dad or at mom's. He wanted to eat at mom's. Charlie spoke about mother not making as much money as before. (There has been a leitmotif during these visits of mother talking to the boys about not keeping the house and maybe having to change schools, not having enough money.) Father encouraged the children to "be good to mom and use those listening ears." Children professed love for dad and look forward to seeing father on Tuesday. *No CI.*

June 23   Again the children profess love to father as they leave. *No CI.*

June 28   Father corrected the children about songs about private parts. They spoke about their dog Hank, apparently a former military dog. *No CI.*

June 30   Charlie said, "Mommy asked me to tell you to give her the birthday and Friday visits." Father responded, "That's a discussion for the adults." *No CI.*

July 2   Father cautioned the children about being gentlemen and not using inappropriate words when addressing Siri on the iPhone. It had been talking about female parts.

July 5   Again the kids greeted their father with hugs and kisses and "I missed you." While playing, Charlie hit his knee and cried. He said "I can't have fun with everything that's going on." Soon Smith hit his knee too. *No CI.* Charlie asked his father about staying away from school. Father stated that the conversation was for his mother and father. *No CI.*

July 12   Again the children greet the father with hugs. Again father encouraged the children to stop using inappropriate jokes. Smith said to his father, "We should spend half the day with you and the other half with Mom." Charlie said, "That would be great." Father cautioned Smith about sexting. *No CI.*

July 14   Again Charlie began to make jokes about female anatomy. When father cautioned him to stop, Charlie persisted. Father gave him a time-out. *No CI.*

July 16   *No CI.*

July 19   Nerf gun and water play. While playing in the backyard Smith bit his tongue and was upset. Father comforted. *CI reported; Smith bumped his head twice on a swing.*

July 21   Again the children were playing with the swings. They appeared to enjoy being with father. Again the children profess, "I love you too, Dad." *No CI.*

July 23   Charlie and Smith enjoyed their time with father watching "Budapest Hotel." *No CI.*

July 28   Father expressed pride at Charlie and Smith growing bigger upon Smith saying he had reached puberty. The children had fun with their father but Charlie said, "My life sucks." *No CI.*

August 2   Charlie said while with father, "I'm the happiest person alive," perhaps referring to getting pumpkin pie. The children appeared to be having fun with their father. Smith got frustrated with an Atari game. He had earlier been frustrated, so he snatched the cartridge out of the game. Father put him in time-out while speaking with Charlie. Charlie later said to his father that he was not having fun at school because he did not have friends and the kids made fun of him. *No CI.*

August 4   Charlie was upset because he said the camp counselors yelled at him. He had complaints about the camp. Smith appeared grumpy and had a tantrum while trying to play hide and seek. He said he wanted to go home. Charlie wanted to continue playing the game. Again there was an exchange of "I love you" and Smith yelled from the car, "I love you, Dad" as he departed. *No CI*

August 11   Charlie, Smith, and father seem happy together. They were looking for a dog on the internet. Father disciplined about respect, Charlie wanted to have a visit tomorrow, he asked why not, and father said he cannot talk about it. *No CI.*

August 14   *NO CI.*

August 16   (AM) Again there were hugs and kisses as the children met their father. Smith informed father "Mom doesn't want us to sing with you. . . . Mom thinks you will hack our location and follow us on GPS." Charlie said, "Mom says if you pull up in a car and try to take us away not to let you." Smith replied, "That's crazy, Dad. You are Dad." His father reassured he would never do that. The boys talked about wanting to create an Instagram account. Father stated for the record Smith could have an Instagram account with father, but Smith was afraid mother would be mad. The children left declaring, "I love you, Dad." *No CI.*

August 16   (PM) There was a communication difficulty and the connection was missed in Van Nuys. Smith asked why he could not stay later. Father replied, "Because time is up for today. It was a mix-up." *No CI.*

August 20   Smith returned from camp to visit father. Smith
                   told his father "It was great seeing you today." He
                   hugged and kissed his father before getting in the
                   car. *No CI.*

August 22   Smith was only present. They went to a soccer
                   store to buy shin guards. Smith complained about
                   being confused about everything going on in his
                   life. He did not want to talk about it. Father held
                   him. Father had a calming influence. *No CI.*

August 26   Smith was the only one present. They had a hard
                   time finding a soccer coach named Jordan. As
                   Smith left, he and father exchanged "I love you."
                   No CI.

August 27   Both boys were present. There was a soccer practice.
                   Charlie told father "Mom said we might be homeless."
                   Smith then said, "I will commit suicide because what's
                   the point." Father said that would never happen.
                   No CI.

August 29   The children joked with father as they knocked on
                   the door, pretending to be salesmen. They greeted
                   their father with kisses and a hug. Charlie informed
                   his father that mother did not want him to have a
                   frozen Gatorade because of plastic residue. Father
                   supported mother and said that "if that's what she
                   said, we need to respect that." Again there were
                   soccer practices. *CI not listed.*

September 1   Both children reported that their mother would
                   not let them bring an Xbox video game from their

home. One or both added, "She says a lot of weird things about security." Again father reprimanded the boys verbally for making drawings about penises. (Why all this sexualized talk from the boys?) The children asked father if they could go to England for a couple of days. Father stated he could not promise that. Charlie continued, "For my birthday we should go to England." Charlie asserted father had said that they would go to England, but Father clarified he did not say that. As they drove away with the monitor, one of the children or both opened the car window and declared, "I love you, Dad." *No CI.*

September 3   The children argued about who pushed whom. Charlie complained that Coach Jordan yells and is mean. Charlie also talked about being sad and confused and he felt things were getting worse. While Charlie was watching "Bob's Burgers," and Smith was playing Minecraft, father fast-forwarded through episodes that he thought were inappropriate talking about swing couples. Again as they drove away the children open the window to yell to father "I love you." *No Cl.*

September 6   Charlie wanted his father to carry him. Both the boys greeted father with hugs. *Cl not listed.*

September 10 There was some kind of team event at Sherman Oaks Park. Charlie ran to his father and embraced him. Smith was already at practice for his team. Charlie and father played with father's phone and seemed to enjoy each other. Smith complained that Father had canceled Tuesday's visit. Father denied that he canceled although Smith said mother told him that father canceled. Father only replied, "Something happened."

September 19   Again this was a time of team sports for the boys. They went to Jim's house. *No CI.*

September 24   Again there were team activities for Charlie. Smith greeted his father with hugs and jokes. Smith and father played together, appeared to be happy. The children again told father that loved him as they went back home. *No CI.*

September 27   Smith was upset and asked his father, "Why does Mom say you did inappropriate things and won't say what?" Father stated they would learn more when they got older. *No CI.*

October 1   Charlie had a football game. Smith wanted his father to arrange for him to have a sleepover at Sonny's house. *No CI.*

2nd INDEPENDENT COURT-ORDERED
PSYCHIATRIC EVALUATION

Requested by counsel for Mother
October, 2019

SUZANNE M. DUPÉE, MD.
A Professional Medical Corporation
Adult, Child & Adolescent and Forensic Psychiatrist

1148 Manhattan Beach, Suite 9
Manhattan Beach, CA 90266
Phone—(310) 335-1288
Fax—(866) 341-8679

Independent Medical Evaluation
PSYCHIATRIC EVALUATION
GREG ELLIS

October 14, 2019

Judge Cochran
Los Angeles Superior Court
111 N. Hill St., Dept. 63
Los Angeles, CA

Your Honor:

I was ordered to conduct a Psychiatric Evaluation of Greg Ellis. Per the order, I received and reviewed all of the medical records prior to evaluating Greg. The psychiatric evaluation was referred by Diana Devilliers of Family Court Services in October 2018. I read the court transcripts regarding the referral for this psychiatric evaluation. My findings are as follows:

SOURCES OF INFORMATION

1. Psychiatric Evaluation of Greg Ellis on September 19, 25, and 30, and October 9, 2019, for a total of seven hours.
2. Interview with Dana Rees on October 8, 2019, for a total of two hours.
3. Minnesota Multiphasic Personality Inventory-2 of Greg Ellis.Personality Assessment Inventory (PAI) of Greg Ellis.
4. Court order for psychiatric evaluation.
5. Transcript of court hearings dated October 19 & 29, 2018.
6. Medical records for Greg Ellis
7. Telephone interviews with Dr.s' and therapists'.

Diagnostic Possibilities:
Axis I: No Diagnosis or Condition on Axis I
Axis II: No Diagnosis on Axis II

DSM 5 DIAGNOSIS

No current evidence of major mental illness
Adjustment Disorder with Depressed Mood – resolved
History of Post Traumatic Stress Disorder

INTERVIEW WITH DANA REES:

Dana said that the DCFS social worker came to visit her the next day after Greg was hospitalized and told her to get a restraining order or DCFS would take the children. She said she got an attorney and was issued an Emergency Protective Order (EPO). She said that she hired security for her house. She said that there was an explosion while she was in the bedroom, and he screamed at her and kicked through the doors. She said he was in the boys' bedroom screaming he loves them. She said that the police came with lights and sirens, and he ran downstairs, and she locked her and the boys in the bedroom. She said that the EPO had expired at 5:00 p.m. that day.

Greg said that he believes that night must have been disturbing for her but it was factually incorrect. He said that the EPO had expired, and up until that time, she had kept him institutionalized. He said he rang the doorbell, and she answered the phone, and he said, "Hey, love, it's me. Let's just please have a conversation." He said she responded by saying, "You need to leave now. I am calling the police." He said that the alarm went off. He said he panicked because he had had little sleep because of the 30-minute monitoring at the Life Healing Center when he was admitted and was stressed and anxious end panicked and just wanted to speak with his wife. He said he had not committed a crime. He said he went to the dining room door and tried opening it, and it was locked. He said the mistake has haunted him, and he tapped out a pane of glass. He said her uncle was there, and he stepped out of the way. He said he walked upstairs and pleaded with Dana to talk to him. He said he walked into the master bedroom, and she sat up saying she was on the phone calling the police, but it was Kevin Berman from the security firm. He said that Kevin heard the conversation. He said that she was screaming, "Get the fuck out, get the fuck out," and "the police are on their way." He said that he thought that he only had limited time and he panicked and went into the boys' bedroom calmly and quickly and told them that he loved them. He said that Smith asked him if his brain was broken and whether he had "bio-polar." He indicated that the children's questions indicated that they were told negative things about him. He said that Charlie said that he was not legally allowed to be there.

Greg said that he has accepted full responsibility for "breaking into" the home, and he would have done things differently. He said the boys were not upset. He said he thought it was best for him to leave and he walked down to the landing, down the stairs and saw his car keys and picked them up and walked out of the front door. He said that Dana was screaming at the boys and slammed the bedroom door and acted like he was some monster. He said the police came along, and he waved them down. He said he had faith in the system at that point, that he was a good person and he could explain what happened. He said they suddenly handcuffed him and put him in the back of a car. He said that Dana claimed that he threatened to physically harm her and kidnap the children, which was untrue. He said that she claimed that he threw a brick through the door and that the children were terrified. He said he was taken to the North Hollywood Police Department and put in solitary confinement in a cell but was told that he was not under arrest. He said he did not get a voice, and she concocted this notion that he came in screaming and yelling. He said he was rational and calmly pleading with the police officers, and they said they believed him, but there was nothing they could do about it.

The reunification therapist reported that the boys stated that they are not afraid of their father at all. Dana said that the monitoring stopped in February 2019 because Smith was really angry with Greg. She said that the monitor sent an email to the attorney saying that until a psychologist for the boys signs off, he was no longer able to do the visits.

Dana said that the first therapist he chose was somebody on the West side, and it was not convenient. They found Marilyn Rand as a reunification therapist but Dana did not agree with her non-safe harbor approach and wouldn't sign the releases.

Dana said that she remains concerned for her and the boys' safety because of Greg's past psychotic breaks (breaking into the house) that terrified her. She believes that he is untreated for Bipolar Disorder. She believes he wants to make her pay and suffer for the divorce. She said that she is afraid for the boys' safety if Greg has unmonitored visits because he might have another psychotic break or say something inappropriate even if he is not psychotic. She said that Smith is under the care of psychiatrists and takes Lexapro and Intuniv (a medication for Attention Deficit Disorder ADHD).

She said that she has a five-year Restraining Order for the three of them and would like future Restraining Orders. She said he has Bipolar Disorder, he needs to be on medication. She said he has done nothing for his problems and not taken any responsibility. She said that there was no abuse to the children beforehand.

CONCLUSIONS & ANALYSIS

This seminal hospitalization set a tragic and fatal spiral of damage to this previously intact and thriving affluent family, despite what appears to be a problematic marriage with little communication. This incident was the definition of a "perfect storm" that has continued to brew for the past four and a half years. The elements of this perfect storm included long-standing marital problems, miscommunication, a propensity for Dana to involve law enforcement based on hearsay and limited information. It should be noted that there does not seem to be any evidence that Greg has or had a drug addiction to cocaine or any other substances. The Del Amo March 15, 2015, hospitalization was noted for Greg's consistent denial of any threats of self-harm or harm to others. It appears that the hearsay allegation of harm to the children was the defining admitting criteria, despite Greg consistently denying any such harm.

The admitting allegations were based solely on hearsay. The records did not note any evidence of psychosis, as alleged by Dana. The only change in mental status was noted as "somewhat irritable" about not being discharged after several days. He refused all medications, and suddenly he was stable for discharge one day after he lost a probable cause hearing that deemed him a danger to others. There is no explanation of this sudden change of mental state for him to be suddenly ready to be discharged. Of note, the Del Amo records contained non-factual information such as that Greg was supported by Federal Disability income. This could be due to the doctor using a template for discharge summaries, but it shows that medical records are not 100% factual.

The sequelae from the Del Anno hospitalization turned Greg and the family's life upside down. The marriage was in jeopardy, his career derailed, he was homeless, and he was not allowed to see the children. It appears that Dana and Greg were not ready to end the marriage shortly after the hospitalization, but Dana insisted Greg seek further intensive treatment to continue the marriage. This led Greg to the Life Healing Center in New Mexico at doctor's suggestion. Greg's treating psychologist indicated he was not discharged against medical advice (AMA) because she was instrumental in liaising Greg leaving the Life Healing Center because he learned that Dana allegedly drained the bank accounts, wanted to end the marriage, and had a protective order against him. Greg clearly used poor judgment when he turned up at the family home unannounced after he left New Mexico. However, Dana and Greg's description of that night were vastly different. There was no restraining order in place, and he was trying to gain access to his own home. I am aware that a restraining order was subsequently granted for one year against Greg after a long trial. Nevertheless, he was taken into custody and ended up at Aurora Charter Oak Hospital. The records from Aurora Charter Oak Hospital indicated he kicked in a glass door and that he might injure the family, but he had no history of violence. Again Greg denied any such danger to others. The hospitalization was on the heels of the first hospitalization at Del Amo. The only reason I can fathom he was admitted to a psychiatric hospital was that he had been recently hospitalized since there was no evidence of any abnormal mental state such a mania, psychosis, or paranoia. Of note, the involuntary hold was discontinued—which is highly unusual for doctors to break a hold. There was no definitive diagnosis from either hospitalization.

After March 2015, there were no further psychiatric incidents until January 2016. This incident was also confounding for the reason he was sent to the hospital. Again he was promptly discharged, and the involuntary hold was discontinued within 24 hours because he was not deemed a danger to himself or others. The final hospitalization occurred May 2016, again under strange circumstances. He was allegedly taken to hospital for depression—which he admits to being deeply depressed about his life circumstances. Again he denied any suicidal ideation. Upon admission, he spoke for 10 minutes and then became volitionally mute. The records indicate that he was catatonic during the brief two-day stay until suddenly he decided to speak and was immediately cleared and discharged.

Catatonia is a serious psychiatric illness and emergency. Catatonia can occur as part of several disorders, including psychotic disorders, mood disorders, and other medical conditions. The course of catatonia does not fit with the history documented in the medical records from the hospital. A patient with such a severe psychiatric condition would not be suddenly ready for discharge within a day or so of onset. There were no other signs or symptoms of catatonia noted in the record, such as behavioral changes, speech changes, and neurological/psychomotor changes in his activity level. The records indicated that Greg told the doctors he was fully aware of everything that had happened at the hospital and that he was overwhelmed by his life circumstances. His description of even being able to state he was aware of everything is inconsistent with a person having catatonia. People suffering from catatonia would likely have little to no memory of their mental state while they are catatonic. Greg was promptly discharged within one day of being described as catatonic. There was no evidence of any manic or psychotic symptoms. The diagnosis was likely given because of his selective mutism that was misdiagnosed as catatonia since catatonia can often be present in a person who is severely psychotic. There was no evidence that he was actually psychotic.

Greg has committed to intense psychotherapy with two doctors—neither of whom diagnosed him with a mood disorder such as Bipolar Disorder or any other major mental illness. He has not taken any psychiatric medication.

Dana seems convinced that Greg has untreated Bipolar Disorder based on the alleged statements from the first treating doctor at Del Amo, where Greg's first psychiatric hospitalization was based solely on hearsay allegations. The first hospitalization set off the effect of bolstering Dana's conviction that her husband is mentally ill while fueling her fears that he is dangerous. The only thing that could be considered "dangerous" was him breaking the glass in the back door to get into his own house. There was no other history in any of the records or from Dana that he has a history of violence. Therefore the notion that he suddenly would present a danger to his children seems to be a reach. Depression, not due to an innate biological predisposition to depression, set in after he was suddenly stripped of the luxuries of the life he lived for decades. He found himself homeless, estranged from his children, unable to work because his reputation was damaged, and ousted by his former community. He simultaneously found himself in a highly contentious and expensive legal battle. Early 2016 was difficult following the holidays. At times his mechanism to deal with the trauma he suffered was to shut down (and be described as "catatonic") so as not to create any further records that could be used against him.

Greg continued to see doctors and threw himself into intensive therapy with several therapists—none of whom ultimately diagnosed any form of Bipolar Disorder. He did not have any substantive period where he took psychotropic medications. He continued to see his children regularly with a professional monitor for three years and tried to make the best of his time with the boys. The visits were suddenly terminated by the monitor, not because of Greg's behavior.

There is no evidence of abnormal or aberrant behavior by Greg reported by the monitors over the years. Despite all the losses he has experienced, Greg remains emotionally strong and abnormally resilient.

Nevertheless, the MMPI-2 profile indicated he is outgoing, social, with a positive self-image. PAI profile was within normal limits and indicated no evidence of mental illness.

It is my opinion with a reasonable degree of medical certainty that Greg suffered depression as a consequence of his life unraveling over the past four years. He does not currently present with any symptoms of depression. He is surprisingly resilient and upbeat but guarded about the legal process—possibly because of this abnormally protracted litigation process. Further he does not suffer from any major mental illness or substance addiction that interferes with his ability to parent his sons.

Greg is an enlightened, psychologically aware man who has been through a lot and has embraced intense psychotherapeutic work that has led him to be able to handle protracted high-conflict litigation and a barrage of negative and damaging descriptions towards him.

I found no evidence that he presents a danger to the children in any way. In fact, the conjoint therapist reported that the boys do not feel their father is dangerous as their mother does.

Further delays in reunification or stalling the legal process should be viewed as containing the estrangement between father and sons.

I declare under penalty of perjury, under the laws of the State of California, that the preceding is true and correct.

Executed this 14th day of October 2019, in Los Angeles, California.

Respectfully submitted,

Suzanne M. Dupée M.D.

Assistant Professor, University of California, Irvine
Board Certified Psychiatrist
Board Certified, Child and Adolescent Psychiatrist
Board Certified, Forensic Psychiatrist

ACKNOWLEDGMENTS

"Blood makes you related—loyalty makes you family."

I extend eternal gratitude to my family members and loyal friends, both new and old, who stood by me and up for me as I grappled with the tumultuous time I endured while navigating the authoritarian maze of family law while endeavoring to complete this book.

Dr. Katrina Wood, Todd Lander, Esq., Dr. Gary David, Adam & Hillary Fogelson, Stephen Fry, David Deluise, Tony Horkins, Alec Baldwin, Andrea Romano, Demi Moore, Tim Reinard, Mirka Royston, Jamie Roberts, Terry Rossio, Terence Carter, Wayne Kasserman, Jay Cohen, Geoffrey Rush, Brian Morton, Michael Epstein, Johnny Depp, Damion & Georgie O'Hare, Clive & Jean Morris, Amanda Patterson, Davis Bauman, Rachel Begley, Andrew Bishop, Aracely Menzoda, Dr. Peter Boghossian, Drew Gomes, Mirka Royston, Stephen Deuters, Ron Carmi, Mike McCormick, Molly K. Olson, Tom Harrison, the Woman of the Two Wolves, the Red Man, Monkey Toes and Smudger.

Some superheroes have capes, some angels have wings. You all have both. You, and many others not mentioned above, all played a part in tending to my torn familial tapestry as I attempted to extend my presence, and the mission of *The Respondent*, further out into the world.

CHILDREN & PARENTS UNITED

A-Team of Family Champions

Family Anchors

Words matter, but alone do not always create meaningful and lasting change. Further, the world does not advance by accident, but rather by design and action. Change of all scale is the result of individuals who are willing to devote time and energy to bringing about a better world. This has eternally been true, and, thus, will be in our time as well. The question then that remains, who in our generation will take the lead? I invite every reader to try to have a positive impact in their community, in whatever way they feel comfortable.

Having experienced the torturous odyssey of divorce court, I personally was inspired to create a powerful and sustainable vehicle that would improve outcomes for children and parents affected by the Family Law cartel. That is why I joined the team behind *The Respondent*. Together, we have formed the non-profit, Children and Parents United (CPU). It is the most recent addition to an ongoing child-advocacy project that provides hope and relief to parents, children, and family members who are being crushed by the legal system. Through family advocacy, mental health awareness, and community action, our mission-driven collaborations will deliver real and meaningful victories for humanity.

The gravest indicator of America's societal health is family breakdown. The United States has the world's highest rate of children living in single parent households. Every single day, 4,000 children lose a parent in family court The tragic and inevitable consequences of the destruction of the traditional family unit include drug abuse, social isolation, and suicide. For example, every year, approximately 800,000 people around the world take their own lives. That's 132 suicides a day. One person every 40 seconds.

In 2019 alone, 50,000 Americans took their own lives. Why does the United States, the richest nation on the planet and only 4 percent of the global population, represent well over 6 percent of the world's suicides?

The reasons are undoubtedly varied, but zero-sum divorce laws are plainly contributing to the morbid parade of shattered lives and senseless deaths in our country. These archaic laws supply little to no relief for parents and children, and low-income households are hit especially hard. Divorced men are eight times more likely to kill themselves than divorced women. The stunning result adds to our nationwide crisis of fatherless homes.

Due to the Covid-19 pandemic and enforced social isolation, children and parents, already under siege from family law, need life-lines more than ever. So how do we provide a safe harbor for families lost at sea and stem the tide of suicide? How can we help families make it through the storm of separation while preventing more trails of suffering and unrecoverable losses?

America's highly adversarial legal system is inimical to healthy human relationships and, as a result, contributes to family breakdown. By now, there is no denying that it routinely compounds the emotional distress of divorce, heaping agony and anguish upon those already enduring a searing experience.

CPU steers our ossified and callous legal system back toward justice, fairness, and fundamental human decency. It uses its significant influence to bring about substantive reforms to existing processes. And where improvements are not possible, CPU harnesses the analytical capabilities and determination of its supporters to forge entirely new, compassionate alternatives. Moreover, CPU promotes and improves the wellbeing of children by delivering key resources for enhancing relationships and reducing conflict. Those affected by family law must be not only heard, but also offered effective support opportunities firmly grounded in evidence-based research.

This work is essential. We will advocate for those falsely accused of domestic violence, champion the presumption of innocence, inspire equal shared parenting, and reduce parental alienation.

Donations to CPU are tax deductible, and 100 percent of monies raised help CPU fund pertinent programs and charitable campaigns, like *The CODE.*

The CODE: Campaign Of Domestic Equality

CPU is committed to drastically changing the family-law system— to make it more humane. But we additionally seek to empower the individuals themselves who are struggling to cope with the family-law system, or even life in general. *The CODE* in turn offers two original and impactful strategies: "The Six Silver Bullets of High Conflict Divorce and "The Magic Ballistics of Family Law War."

The CODE e-book is full of tips, insights, and secrets for navigating the trauma of family separation. **Visit www.therespondent.com and input the code *bringthathorizon* at check out to receive your free copy.**

Share #TheCODE to provide families immediate relief, help provide hope, reduce suicide, diminish social isolation, and reform zero-sum divorce laws.

Losing my own father as a boy, then being deprived of contact with my sons—who provided my entire life with purpose and meaning—forced me to heal the parts of my soul that were damaged. I did not have a book like *The Respondent*, a campaign like *The CODE*, or an organization like CPU. And so it took many years of grueling recovery work to fully accept the indifference of my former spouse and manage the excruciating separation from my boys, the inescapability of the trauma—and to do so without bitterness or anger. That psychological journey required connecting with the parts of myself that were hidden in the shadows.

The collapse of my emotional and psychological house of cards had been long overdue. But in its wake, I transcended material wealth to discover that only emotional health made one truly rich. I was finally a man of genuine prosperity. I became a man of meaning.

We are all capable of admitting our failures. I accept full responsibility, as I must, for the part I played in the breakdown of my family. Dana and I were good parents to our sons. I am grateful to her for the twenty years we spent together, and for gifting our family two amazing children. I am not driven by bitterness or anger toward her, or those in the legal system who participated in and profited from making our boys fatherless.

My time with my father was cut short, as was mine with my boys. The glorious, multicolored memories with my sons continuously cycle through my mind. They are my non-perishable keepsakes now.

I lost the battle to remain a father. Now I venture forth with deeper meaning and renewed purpose: to help other fathers, children and parents remain united.

To find out more about *The Respondent* video podcast series, to donate to CPU, or to receive a free copy of *The CODE* e-book, please visit www.therespondent.com.

GLOSSARY

alive coach—A philosophical and phenomenological guide to the application of #TheCode.

allegation—a claim that someone has done something illegal or wrong, typically made without proof.

child support—Money that a non-custodial parent pays to the custodial parent to cover costs for the child/children.

court order—A legal decision made by a court.

defamation—The action of damaging the good reputation of someone; slander or libel.

defendant—The person against whom legal papers are filed—also known as the respondent.

dissolution—Another word for divorce.

divorce—The legal termination of a marriage relationship.

domestic violence—Physical or threats of abuse occurring between members of the same household.

emotional containment—The capacity to stay present and control emotions in a way that does not overwhelm.

emotional projections—Displacements of emotions we don't want to feel.

enforcement agencies—A government agency responsible for enforcing laws.

ex-parte—An emergency hearing in family law.

female toxicity—A female act of using gender to obtain certain privileges.

incarceration—The state of being confined in prison.

interrogate—To examine by questions. To question formally.

joint legal custody—Both parents share the right to make important decisions about a child/children's welfare.

legal custody—The parent who has legal custody has the right to make important decisions about their child's welfare such as health care, religion and education.

mediator—A person who attempts to find resolution between two parties involved in a conflict.

neuroplasticity—The brain's ability to reorganize and regenerate itself by positive thinking, compassion and nurture.

no-fault divorce—A divorce in which the dissolution of a marriage does not require evidence of wrongdoing by either party.

paternity—Legal confirmation of fatherhood. Paternity must be determined before a court can order child support.

plaintiff—Someone who brings legal action in a court of law.

petition—A formal application made to a court in writing that requests action on a certain matter.

petitioner—A person who gathers signatures for psychological conditioning initiatives to present to an authority for a particular cause.

phenomenology—The study of phenomena (the existence of anything that can be seen, felt, tasted) and how these are experienced.

physical custody—This refers to where the children live on a regular basis. It can be shared by both parents or granted to just one.

mindwellness—More than mental health—positivity and acknowledging that each sense contributes to mental wellness.

reputation savage—Someone who works tirelessly to reframe reality and psychologically recondition the beliefs of others.

respondent—A person who is called upon to issue a response to a communication made by a petitioner. The term is used in legal contexts and in psychological conditioning.

restraining order—A temporary court order issued to prohibit an individual from doing something. Usually issued in conjunction with domestic violence or custody disputes.

scapegoat—A person blamed for the faults of others, especially for reasons of expediency.

silver bullets—Simple, seemingly magical solutions to difficult problems.

toxic masculinity—Used in academic discussions referring to cultural norms that lead to harm to society and to men themselves

visitation—The time a noncustodial parent spends with his or her child(ren).

5150 hold—To be placed in this involuntary 72-hour hold, a person must be considered a danger to themselves or others.

BIBLIOGRAPHY

American SPCC. "Child Abuse And Father Figures: Which Kind Of Families Are Safest To Grow Up In?" Published August 16, 2017. https://americanspcc.org/2017/08/16/child-abuse-father-figures-kind-families-safest-grow/

Arnold, Nathan. "Dads Represent 85% Of Child Support Providers, Pay More Than Female Payer," *Dads Divorce*, 2018. https://dadsdivorce.com/articles/dads-represent-85-of-child-support-providers-pay-more-than-female-payers.

Baskerville, Stephen, *Taken Into Custody: The War Against Fathers, Marriage, and the Family*, 2007.

Bourget, Dominique MD, Jennifer Grace, MA, and Laurie Whitehurst, PhD. "A Review of Maternal and Paternal Filicide." *The Journal of the American Academy of Psychiatry and the Law* 35, no. 1 (2007): 74—82. http://jaapl.org/content/jaapl/35/1/74.full.pdf.

Breiding, M.J., J. Chen, and M.C. Black. Intimate Partner Violence in the United States—2010. Atlanta: National Center for Injury Prevention and Control, Centers for Disease Control and Prevention, 2014. https://cdc.gov/violenceprevention/pdf/cdc_nisvs_ipv_report_2013_v17_single_a.pdf.

Cancian, Maria et al. "Who Gets Custody Now? Dramatic Changes in Children's Living Arrangements After Divorce." *Demography* 51, (2014): 1381–1396. https://doi.org/10.1007/s13524-014-0307-8.

Castillo, Stephanie. "Evolutionary Psychology's Effect On Divorce." *Medical Daily*. August 24, 2015. https://medicaldaily.com/evolutionary-psychologys-effect-divorce-married-women-carry-historical-baggage-end-349270.

CDC/National Center for Health Statistics "Attention Deficit Hyperactivity Disorder (ADHD)." Last reviewed April 20, 2020. https://cdc.gov/nchs/fastats/adhd.htm.

Chokshi, Niraj. "Workplace Deaths in 2015 Reached Six-Year High." *New York Times*, December 20, 2016. https://nytimes.com/2016/12/20/us/workplace-deaths-2015.html.

Dubner, Stephen J. "The True Story of the Gender Pay Gap." *Freakonomics*, January 7, 2016. https://freakonomics.com/podcast/the-true-story-of-the-gender-pay-gap-a-new-freakonomics-radio-podcast

Durose, Matthew R. et al. *Family Violence Statistics*, Washington: U S Department of Justice, 2005. https://bjs.gov/content/pub/pdf/fvs03.pdf.

Farrell, Warren, PhD and John Gray, PhD. *The Boy Crisis*. Dallas: BenBella Books, 2018.

Fiebert, Martin S. "References Examining Assaults By Women On Their Spouses Or Male Partners: An Annotated Bibliography." California State University. Last updated June 2012. https://web.csulb.edu/~mfiebert/assault.htm.

Geiger A.W. and Kim Parker. "Gender Gains—and Gaps—in the U S " Pew Research Center, March 15, 2018. https://pewresearch.org/fact-tank/2018/03/15/for-womens-history-month-a-look-at-gender-gains-and-gaps-in-the-u-s.

Grall, Timothy. *Custodial Mothers and Fathers and Their Child Support*. Maryland: U S Census Bureau, 2016. https://census. gov/content/dam/Census/library/publications/2016/demo/P60-255.pdf.

Henry, Meghan et al. *The 2018 Annual Homeless Assessment Report (AHAR) to Congress* The U S Department of Housing and Urban Development, 2018. https://www.wpr.org/sites/default/files/2018-ahar-part-1-compressed.pdf

Heritage Foundation. "The Importance of Dads in an Increasingly Fatherless America." June 15, 2018. https://heritage.org/marriage-and-family/commentary/the-importance-dads-increasingly-fatherless-america.

Jerabek, Ilona. "The Subjectivity Of Honesty: New Study Reveals Gender Differences In Views of Dishonesty," *Cision*, June 17, 2017. https://prweb.com/releases/2017/06/prweb14410566.htm.

Julian, Kate. "What Happened to American Childhood?" *The Atlantic*, April 17, 2020. https://www.theatlantic.com/magazine/archive/2020/05/childhood-in-an-anxious-age/609079.

Livingston, Gretchen. "The Changing Profile of Unmarried Parents." Pew Research Center. April 25, 2018. https://pewsocialtrends. org/2018/04/25/the-changing-profile-of-unmarried-parents.

Livingston, Gretchen and Kim Parker. "8 facts about American dads." Pew Research Center. June 12, 2019. https://www.pewresearch. org/fact-tank/2019/06/12/fathers-day-facts.

Martin, Rachel. "Who Fails To Pay Child Support? Moms, At A Higher Rate Than Dads." *NPR*, March 1, 2015. https://www.npr. org/2015/03/01/389945311/who-fails-to-pay-child-support-moms-at-a-higher-rate-than-dads.

Miller, Laura. "A Twisted Fairy Tale About Toxic Masculinity." *New Yorker*, December 31, 2018. https://newyorker.com/magazine/2019/01/07/a-twisted-fairy-tale-about-toxic-masculinity.

Monnier, Jen. "Moms Show Gender Bias Against Emotional Expression in Boys. But Why?" *Fatherly*, January 10, 2020. https://www.fatherly.com/health-science/moms-gender-bias-boys-emotions.

National Father Initiative. "The Proof Is In: Father Absence Harms Children." Last updated 2020. https://fatherhood.org/father-absence-statistic.

National Institute of Mental Health. "Suicide." Last updated April, 2019. https://nimh.nih.gov/health/statistics/suicide.shtml.

Perry, Mark J. "Women earned majority of doctoral degrees in 2017 for 9th straight year and outnumber men in grad school 137 to 100." AEI, October 3, 2018. https://aei.org/carpe-diem/women-earned-majority-of-doctoral-degrees-in-2017-for-9th-straight-year-and-outnumber-men-in-grad-school-137-to-100-2.

Peterson, Andrea. *On Edge*. Manhattan: Crown Publishing, 2017.

Press Association. "Women in their 20s earn more than men of same age, study finds." *The Guardian*, August 29, 2015. https://theguardian.com/money/2015/aug/29/women-in-20s-earn-more-men-same-age-study-finds

R29 Brand Experiences. "What The Modern American Family Looks Like—By The Numbers." *Refinery, 29* January 17, 2018. https://www.refinery29.com/en-us/women-breadwinners-household-income-family-impact

Rosenfeld, Michael J. "Who wants the Breakup? Gender and Breakup in Heterosexual Couples" in *Social Networks and the Life Course: Integrating the Development of Human Lives and Social Relational Networks*, edited by Duane F. Alwin, Diane Felmlee and Derek Kreager, 221-43. Springer International Publishing, 2018. http://web.stanford.edu/~mrosenfe/Rosenfeld_gender_of_breakup.pdf.

Rosenstock, Linda, M.D., M.P.H, Stephen Joseph, M.D., M.P.H. "National Mortality Profile of Active Duty Personnel in the U S Armed Forces: 1980-1993." CDC, 2012. https://cdc.gov/niosh/docs/96-103/pdfs/96-103.pdf?id=10.26616/NIOSHPUB96103.

Sommers, Christina Hoff. "School Has Become Too Hostile to Boys." *Time*, August 19, 2013. https://ideas.time.com/2013/08/19/school-has-become-too-hostile-to-boys/.

Stewart, William, "Teacher stereotyping means higher marks for girls." *TES*, March 5, 2015. https://tes.com/news/teacher-stereotyping-means-higher-marks-girls-says-oecd.

Tjaden, Patricia and Nancy Thoennes. *Extent, Nature, and Consequence of Intimate Partner Violence.* Washington: Department of Justice, November 2000. https://ncjrs.gov/pdffiles1/nij/183781.pdf.

Tjaden, Patricia and Nancy Thoennes. *Full Report of the Prevalence, Incidence, and Consequences of Violence Against Women.* Washington: Department of Justice, November 2000. https://ncjrs.gov/pdffiles1/nij/181867.pdf.

Turkat, Ira Daniel, Ph.D. "Divorce-Related Malicious Mother Syndrome," *The Journal Of Family Violence*, 10, No. 3 (1995): 253-264. http://fact.on.ca/Info/pas/turkat01.htm#:~:text=The%20proposed%20definition%20encompasses%20four,malicious%20actions%20against%20the%20father

United States Census Bureau. "The Majority of Children Live With Two Parents, Census Bureau Reports." Released on November 17, 2016. https://census.gov/newsroom/press-releases/2016/cb16-192.html#:~:text=During%20the%201960%2D2016%20period,from%203%20to%204%20percent.

University of Michigan. "Study Finds Large Gender Disparities In Federal Criminal Cases." Published November 16, 2012. http://law. http://law.umich.edu/newsandinfo/features/Pages starr_gender_disparities.aspx?fbclid=IwAR0iOsy0WBDTG 481ggOoV5tIy8yugIzC5ARyaODmidhlyew6IUiaufljY5g.

Wang, Wendy. "Who Cheats More? The Demographics of Infidelity in America." Institute for Family Studies, January, 2018. https://ifstudies.org/blog/who-cheats-more-the-demographics-of-cheating-in-america.

Whitaker, Daniel J. et al. "Differences in Frequency of Violence and Reported Injury Between Relationships With Reciprocal and Nonreciprocal Intimate Partner Violence," *American Journal of Public Health* 97, no. 5 (May 1, 2007): 941-947. https://doi.org/10.2105/AJPH.2005.079020.

Wikipedia. "Sex differences in crime." Last edited 6 August, 2020. https://en.wikipedia.org/wiki/Sex_differences_in_crime.

Willett, Beverly. "What fifty years of no-fault divorce has gotten us." *Washington Examiner*, August 13, 2019. https://washingtonexaminer.com/opinion/op-eds/what-fifty-years-of-no-fault-divorce-has-gotten-us.

Wright D.B., Skagerberg E.M. "Measuring Empathizing and Systemizing with a Large US Sample." *PLOS ONE* 7 no. 2 (2012). https://doi.org/10.1371/journal.pone.0031661.

Young, Cathy. "Boys, Feminism, and Empathy." *Arc Digital*. February 1, 2020. https://arcdigital.media/boys-feminism-and-empathy-748cdb9e23b1.

Young, Cathy. "The Surprising Truth About Women and Violence." *Time*. June 25, 2014. https://time.com/2921491/hope-solo-women-violence.

ABOUT THE AUTHOR

Photo by Dani Brubaker

GREG ELLIS, raised and toughened in the seaside fish-and-chip shops and smoky video game arcades of rough-and-tumble Southport, England, mastered the Rubik's cube at twelve, held the world record for Pac-Man at thirteen, performed a lead role in a West End musical at fourteen, had a number one single on the pop charts at fifteen, left school at sixteen and home at seventeen. He has skydived from 10,000 feet above the earth, completed one Ironman and ten triathlons, won the South Beach Triathlon, made the cut at the BMW golf championships, competed against ski legends Franz Klammer and Marc Giardelli, played doubles with twelve-time Grand Slam champion Mark Woodforde at Wimbledon on finals Sundays, performed for Prince, Michael Jackson, Princess Diana, HRH Queen Elizabeth ll at three Royal Command Performances, written songs with Robbie Williams, sung the American national anthem at New York Rangers and Oakland A's games, a duet with Lorrie Morgan at the Las Vegas Hilton, and a live-television rendition of "Halfway Down the Stairs" with Kermit the Frog on the red carpet at the *Pirates of the Caribbean* premiere.

He has taught phenomenological classes to orphans born with HIV in India, storytelling at the Parva Slum School in Jaipur, practiced shamanic rituals with the Cherokee Nation, purification sweat lodges with the Skidi Tribe, studied affect theory with epistemologist Dr. Gary David, and created the Mindwell initiative with the Global Wellness Institute. He's a published author, TV director, Annie Award–nominated voice artist and Emmy Award®–nominated actor who has appeared in Oscar-winning movies, directed Hollywood superstars, produced and written television shows and commercials, performed leading stage roles in original Andrew Lloyd Webber and Cameron Mackintosh musicals in London's West End and Las Vegas, voiced cartoon characters for movies, TV series, cartoons, over 120 video games and toys, and has over twenty action figures of characters he's portrayed, and has recorded multiple albums, singles and soundtracks.

Greg's major motion picture film credits include billion-dollar franchises like the *Pirates of the Caribbean* series, and *Titanic, Star Trek, Mr. & Mrs. Smith*, and *Beowulf.* TV credits include *24, The X-Files, CSI, Dexter, NCIS, Hawaii Five-O*, and more. Under his production company banner, Monkey Toes, Greg has written and directed projects for Kiefer Sutherland and Stephen Fry, and produced and directed multiple commercials. He hosts the video podcast series *The Voices in My Head, Wiser Life Practices, Quillette Narrated*, and *The Respondent.*

Greg's online Alive Coaching improvement program, www.thealiveinstitute.com, helps people address past problems and improve their future, and his official website, www.realgregellis.com, provides information on all of Greg's projects, while the multimedia child advocacy series www.therespondent.com aims to inspire family champions through the charity CPU: Children and Parents United.

Follow @ellisgreg, @TheRespondent, and @MonkeyToes on Twitter, @realgregellis on Instagram, Monkey Toes Studio on YT. Join The Respondent, Monkey Toes Studio and CPU Clubs on the Clubhouse app @ge, and subscribe to The Respondent on Substack.

ALSO BY GREG ELLIS

POETRY

The Knewledge
A Book of Poetry

PROSE

NoThing In Between
A Pocket Oracle of Philosophical Quotes

Lightning Source UK Ltd.
Milton Keynes UK
UKHW011941060821
388460UK00011B/748/J